THE POWER OF

PERSISTENT PLANNING

THE POWER OF
PERSISTENT PLANNING

A Review of Successful Financial Planning Strategies

DOUGLAS B. GROSS, CFP®, MBA

Published by Advantage, Charleston, South Carolina.
Member of Advantage Media Group.

ADVANTAGE is a registered trademark and the Advantage colophon is a trademark of Advantage Media Group, Inc.

Printed in the United States of America.

ISBN: 978-1-59932-704-4
LCCN: 2016950635

Book design by Katie Biondo.

This publication is designed to provide accurate and authoritative information in regard to the subject matter covered. It is sold with the understanding that the publisher is not engaged in rendering legal, accounting, or other professional services. If legal advice or other expert assistance is required, the services of a competent professional person should be sought.

Advantage Media Group is proud to be a part of the Tree Neutral® program. Tree Neutral offsets the number of trees consumed in the production and printing of this book by taking proactive steps such as planting trees in direct proportion to the number of trees used to print books. To learn more about Tree Neutral, please visit **www.treeneutral.com.**

Advantage Media Group is a publisher of business, self-improvement, and professional development books. We help entrepreneurs, business leaders, and professionals share their Stories, Passion, and Knowledge to help others Learn & Grow. Do you have a manuscript or book idea that you would like us to consider for publishing? Please visit **advantagefamily.com** or call **1.866.775.1696.**

TABLE OF CONTENTS

ACKNOWLEDGMENTS

I'm very thankful for having had the opportunity to serve so many wonderful clients over the years. Their thoughtfulness and understanding make it a joy to be of service. Sometimes when a client asks a question, I ask myself why they want to know that, but almost inevitably, by researching it, we learn something that is a benefit to them and to others! Their willingness to share very personal information gives us a unique window into their situations and greatly helps us to be of service. We learn from every client, sometimes right away and sometimes later, but by listening closely we always benefit as do they.

Some clients I want to give special recognition to are Leo and Dianna Fox and Bruce and Joyce Herbert. Each have been clients for a decade or more, and working with them has led to all kinds of learning, adventure, and joy. The stories here are not about them, but my work with them has truly changed me and my business over time.

I'd like to also thank my employees, past and present. Working together, we consistently come up with better solutions than any one of us would individually. Their desire to serve clients and their ongoing seeking and questioning all lead to better outcomes! My employees' attention to all the details from tax lots to money transfers and a thousand other things makes it all work.

Also, I'd like to extend my sincere appreciation to Robert Sheasley, who was instrumental in taking this book from a concept to a living, breathing book. He encouraged me to tell my stories and had a wonderful way at helping me bring them to life.

My peers in the industry have been more than just friends; they are confidants and wonderful resources. I'd like to recognize in particular:

- my peers on the Financial Planning Association of Michigan Board;
- friends at Raymond James both at headquarters and fellow advisors;
- local attorneys and CPAs who help us to guide our clients and complete the details like estate plans and tax returns, especially Warren Widmayer, Michael McCarthy, and Kirk Johnson;
- Capitas Financial and all the help they have provided us on complex insurance issues;
- Steve O'Hara, Todd Sanford, Fernando Erenata, Melissa Joy, Denis Smirnov, David Sisemore, Tom Baughman, and Charlie Waterhouse; and finally,
- my father, who was the inspiration for the wealth worksheet, my mother, for her support, my wife and editor Sabrina, who looked at all the details, my daughters, Natalie, Audrey, and Lily who are a great source of joy every day.

IS THIS BOOK FOR YOU?

In the pages ahead, you will find practical advice for people who have achieved significant financial success: the affluent entrepreneur, in particular, and the high-end corporate employee. This book is of particular interest to those who are approaching retirement and wonder what they should be doing instead of simply making more money and accumulating more stuff. Younger readers on the way to success also will find essential information here on laying the foundations to improve their finances and their quality of life.

Successful people lead complicated lives, trying to keep a lot of balls in the air. They need, at various times, accountants, attorneys, and other professionals to help manage it all. Above all, they need a coach—a coordinator who will make sure that everyone and everything works in concert and in their best interest. Good advice takes more than a phone call. It requires a long-term relationship. It is in that capacity that I serve my clients. I am looking for the relationship of fifteen or twenty or thirty years to help people make the right decisions over the long term and avoid making the big mistakes.

Almost all of my clients have built their wealth by spending less than they make. They have focused on saving money. As a result, they have a great deal of flexibility in their retirement. If they wanted a second home, they could buy it with cash. If they wanted to increase their giving to charities, they could do so.

If this describes you, consider how fortunate you are to have hit the home run. Certainly you would like to see your children achieve a similar standard of living by cultivating the savings habit early in life and learning to live below their means. You can teach them, by your example, how they can help themselves.

The prevailing wisdom among farmers is: "Never eat your seed corn." Life is unpredictable, and so we need to store up for a prosperous future. Living modestly has many benefits. You invite less stress into your life. You can provide for those you love. And perhaps the greatest benefit is that your children observe your decisions and come to understand that it is not all about money.

Saving isn't about hoarding money for a rainy day. More than anything else, money provides freedom: freedom to be charitable, freedom to travel, and freedom to change jobs or start a new company or venture.

Money is the end result of the hard work, expertise, good fortune, and thrift, and it is a tangible benefit that you can pass on. As a financial planner for many families like yours, I understand the value of a dollar—I also understand the value of the relationship. I help families keep it all in perspective as they pursue a life of richness.

I invite you now to join me on a journey of understanding. You have made it. You have built your wealth and a lifestyle that pleases you—and you want to keep it that way.

INTRODUCTION

POWER OF PERSISTENCE

Nothing in the world can take the place of persistence.
Persistence and determination alone are omnipotent.

CALVIN COOLIDGE

I ron is forged in a blast furnace under extreme heat. Every business goes through similar experiences over time. For me, the dot-com meltdown of 2000 and the financial crisis of 2008 were those experiences. Each one challenged the foundations of my business and my investment and financial planning processes.

Experience and training prepared me to deal with those challenges. Let me share with you some of the lessons of my past that have played a significant role in my pursuit of success. I want to give you a glimpse of how I was able to build the foundations that have helped me to serve my clients well.

At about the turn of the millennium, when I was making steady progress in building my financial planning practice, we moved from a house in town to a house on a pond. It didn't take long, in a Michigan winter, for that shallow pond to freeze into what appeared to be an ideal skating rink in our backyard.

"Let's try it out," I told our girls, Natalie and Audrey, who were twelve and ten at the time. Our third daughter, Lily, was just three. I hadn't ice skated since I was a kid and only a couple times even then.

1

"Maybe we could have some fun skating," I told them, "or we could even play hockey."

And so we bought some inexpensive skates and set up a few cones out on the ice. We pretended that we were masters of our makeshift rink. To anyone observing, I'm sure that we appeared somewhat less so. Nonetheless, our hockey outings soon became our favorite pastime whenever the ice was thick enough.

The girls began to invite their friends over, and before long we would have fifteen or twenty kids out on the pond in the evening, playing hockey. Then my wife and I began inviting people, too, and on weekend days we would often host a neighborhood hockey game, with players ages six to sixty having a great time together.

It was party central on this pond and a wonderful opportunity for a variety of people to connect with one another. In wintertime, neighbors might not see each other for three or four months as they huddle in their homes. And yet there we were, all together, skating and laughing and talking, enjoying the outdoors and bonding with our neighbors.

The Human Touch

I did not work on a neighborhood ice rink just because I am an avid hockey fan—I would much rather be a participant than a spectator. And I'm not just talking about participating in sports. I'm talking about participating in life—that is what I really wanted to teach my daughters. On those cold days and evenings, we were warm. The bonfires helped, of course, but this was the warmth that came from people getting to know one another. This was the warmth of the human touch. We found joy in the competition and also in the camaraderie.

I understand this about myself: I was made to be a participant in life. It is important to me to extend a hand to others, to get to know my fellow travelers. I am most interested in helping others and building relationships, and as such I have found my niche as a financial planner, helping people design a prosperous and fulfilling future.

I began my career, however, attempting to follow in the footsteps of my father, Charles Gross, a successful accountant. I admired him, and I thought I wanted to be just like him, but I was unhappy as a certified public accountant (CPA). I wanted something different. Rather than working on auditing and tax preparation, I wanted to examine the overall blueprint of where my clients were headed in life, how they were pursuing their dreams, and what it would take for them to get there. My career evolved beyond the numbers and into the relationships.

When I play hockey, I try to score. I almost always want to be on the offense. I'm willing to play defense, and I recognize its importance, but I want to make things happen—and you can't win the game unless you put points up on the board.

As an accountant, I did not feel that I had the opportunity to improve clients' situations in a way that was the best match for my abilities. I felt that I was just reporting numeric values, and I wanted a more proactive approach. Accounting is a noble occupation, and its practitioners are the utmost professionals. They certainly offer their clients sound tax advice that makes a major difference, and some of my best work as a financial planner has been in relationships with other CPAs as we collaborate on how best to save money for our clients.

As a young accountant, however, I had not reached that level of trusted advisor. Experienced and talented accountants certainly provide proactive service, but you don't generally get to do that at the entry level, where I was. I recognized that, to be happy, I would need to engage in more creative thinking and work not just with numbers but also more closely with people.

Lessons in Perseverance

My path as a participant was a study in evolution. In my youth, playing sports was a challenge for me. I was marginally coordinated and not particularly skilled. I tried out for football in eighth grade and promptly broke my leg. When I tried out for basketball in my freshman year of high school, I was in the bottom 10 percent of fifty boys who wanted to be on the team. Most games I sat on the bench and recorded statistics. The coach put me in during the last two minutes of one game because our team was ahead by over fifty points.

I determined that my best option was in intramural sports, where I would be able to compete instead of riding the bench. In football I became the intramural quarterback—not because I had a wonderful arm or speed but because I had a good sense of what was happening, where the opportunities were, and which plays to call on short notice in the huddle. I continued that participation pattern in college. In one of my last intramural games, we were leading against the team that was at the top of the league. With a minute to go, all we needed was a first down, and then we could run down the clock. I have no idea why I decided to go back to throw. My pass landed right in the hands of an opponent, who raced in for a touchdown. It was a defeat snatched from the jaws of victory.

This was one more sports experience that taught me to persevere. Life is like a marathon, and we need to keep our stride if we are to succeed. We need to stay in the race. For many of us, the best lessons are the times when we do not succeed. We need to keep making the plays. I was never content on the bench. I became determined to be a participant, not an observer.

Today, in my financial planning practice, my colleagues and I continue to cultivate that attitude. To manage clients' portfolios requires active engagement and decision making. It is most certainly a contact sport, and I prefer it that way. In no way did my youthful frustrations dissuade me from an athletic life. I remain an active participant in tennis, ice hockey, sailing, racquetball, rowing, and biking. I seek to play sports that challenge me, that are aerobic, and that give me an opportunity to satisfy that ongoing drive to compete. Yes, I like to win, but the real joy comes from competing. I am forever seeking to do better, to learn more. Winning is transitory, but striving and persisting are a constant. That is a lesson for sports and a lesson for investing.

When I was in college, seven friends and I decided to go on a hiking trip out West. We planned to start with a five-day hike up in the San Juan Mountains near Durango, Colorado, climbing to twelve thousand feet, going over a pass, and back down. At ten thousand feet, six of us, including me, turned back because we had altitude sickness. Later, we attempted the Longs Peak climb, but we were caught in an August snowstorm and needed to halt that trip, too. As a young man who was very interested in taking on physical challenges, this trip was very disappointing.

Thirty years later, I returned to the area. Two friends and I decided to see how many fourteen-thousand-foot peaks we could conquer in a week. We climbed four—and the last one was Longs Peak, the mountain that had frustrated me as a student. It took three decades, but the victory was mine.

Young people sometimes allow frustrations to slow them down, and I did have much to learn in those intervening years about perseverance and resolve. Life brings challenges to all of us. It is how we respond to those challenges, and the actions we take, that help determine our future. Today I know this without a doubt: If you really work at something, you can do it. We don't necessarily get it right the first time, and we can be grateful for that because it is how we learn and how we grow.

> I learned early in life that the richness of life is found in adventure. Adventure calls on all the faculties of mind and spirit. It develops self-reliance and independence. Life then teems with excitement. But man is not ready for adventure unless he is rid of fear. For fear confines him and limits his scope. He stays tethered by strings of doubt and indecision and has only a small and narrow world to explore. This book may help others to use the mountains to prepare for adventure.

This is a passage from *Of Men and Mountains* by former Supreme Court Justice William O. Douglas. The book is about his time as a youth, hiking in the mountains of the Pacific Northwest in the 1920s.

Building for the Future

Before I was a financial planner, I was a part-time landlord. My wife, Sabrina, and I were determined to save money for our daughters to go to college, but we couldn't figure out how to do it. I ran the math, and when I saw how much money I would need to save every month, I realized that there just was not enough room in our budget to set aside what would be required. I was working at the time as a pricing manager for a book-printing company, Malloy Lithographing, which today is Edwards Brothers Malloy.

Putting our heads together, Sabrina and I saw an opportunity to purchase an income-producing rental property. It was four units, which we converted into five by creatively using some space under the roof. Over the course of two years, we rehabilitated every unit. I took out walls. I rerouted plumbing. I put in windows. Not only did we realize some sweat equity, but I also learned a variety of construction and handyman skills, hiring professionals when necessary. What's more, I learned the management skills required to deal with tenants.

Above all, I continued to gain confidence. This was a challenge, and I could make it happen. We were successful with that venture and began to put more money aside. We had made this work, and I realized that I did not need to work for others. I could start my own financial planning business using my skills as a CPA and my master's in business from the University of Michigan. For many people, entrepreneurship is intimidating. It is quite a leap to leave a secure job and enter a world filled with uncertainties. The landlord experience encouraged me. I knew that I had the ability to take on a challenge and turn it into profit.

A few months after I launched my financial advisor business, we sold the rental property. It was a fairly quick transition. I needed to spend my time on my clients, not on rental property. I needed to spend my time building and managing portfolios. I needed to build a business and serve clients.

A Change in Course

Until now, you have likely been charting your own course toward retirement, and the earlier you start, the better. It is important both to save money and to identify what you want to do with it. For most people, this process becomes an imperative in their fifties. Identifying what you want to do with it can be a challenge for many couples.

As you approach the end of your working years, you are entering a new phase of life, and the rules feel quite different. You have spent decades striving to accumulate money. Now, the focus must begin to turn to protecting those gains. Unless you adjust to that reality, your portfolio and your sense of security may suffer.

The fundamental fear that retirees express, whether they have accumulated millions or more modest savings, is concern about having enough money for the rest of their lives. They come to us concerned about whether they have accumulated enough resources, not only to carry on day by day but also to do the things they have dreamed of doing.

People often tell me that they just don't talk to anybody else about these matters. Money feels like private territory, even within the family. Sometimes, even spouses and partners are not able to address this critical challenge. They may talk about it eventually but fail to come to agreement, which leads to conflict and makes it less likely that they will be able to talk heart to heart. Having a third person to help navigate these sensitive topics may be what makes the difference. A professional assisting in organizing, focusing, and addressing these issues is very important. Many people simply don't like to talk about money, and a professional guide will ensure that you do. For many of us, a financial advisor helps ensure that we address issues rather than putting them off. As you head into retirement, clarity is essential. To achieve clarity requires discussion and work.

In general, as you approach your retirement, you should gradually become more conservative with your portfolio. Your portfolio will need to provide you with a sustainable lifetime income. Certainly you need to maintain an overall balance, but now one with a more protective stance. You will want to take fewer risks than you did when you were younger. You had years to recover then if investments went awry. Now, the dips of the Dow no longer feel like a good time to buy. Investment volatility is no longer your friend.

A Spectrum of Success

My clients are primarily of retirement age or approaching it. Most have been very successful entrepreneurs, business executives, or health and academic professionals. They have been highly successful; if they are employees of a company, they have risen to the upper ranks. Those who still are working are at the peak of their careers and are well rewarded. They are devoting extensive hours to their careers, and their day-to-day responsibilities tend to be all-consuming. I have a number of clients who worked in the pharmaceutical industry, in sales or drug development. Many are in Michigan, but I also have numerous clients around the country—from Florida to California and in the Northeast.

These clients are people who are making good money, have built and continue to build a substantial portfolio, and are seeking someone to manage it. They come to us with a wide variety of complicated situations. They are looking at diversification of their portfolios, particularly those who have received stock options and are concerned about the concentration of their wealth. In general, they need someone to help them with the management of the money that they have accumulated. Many of them do not have the time or the inclination to deal with the details themselves, and so they are looking for a coach to oversee their finances and help them make sense of it all. They are concerned that they may make mistakes that would cost them dearly.

Those are the sorts of individuals who will benefit greatly from reading this book—and that may very well describe you. If you seek guidance in managing your financial assets, you will find a wealth of information in these pages. You will also find stories about what other people much like you have experienced on their journeys. You will read about their successes and their challenges. Details have been changed to protect their identities, but the fundamental facets of planning and investing that are core to the stories remain.

Through stories, we gain understanding and learn valuable lessons. Why are folks today still so fascinated by tales of the Titanic? Why are we so interested in reading about the hubris of a captain who put his ship in peril trying to cross the Atlantic in record time? You can shake your head and tell yourself that you never would have taken such a risk—yet many investors have often done something similar. It is our goal to help you to get from Southampton, England, to New York while steering clear of the icebergs. You can reach your destination in style, and you don't have to go at maximum speed.

A Guide to Achieving Wealth and Living Well

This book is for people who want to better understand how comprehensive financial planning can help guide them through life. It is not for those who simply want hot tips or are looking for the highest possible return to beat some benchmark or another. How you should invest your money depends greatly upon who you are and the situations that you are facing in life. Therefore, you will not find specific investment advice herein. You will learn more about blocking and tackling than about offensive plays. The book is not just about financial planning but also about other important parts of life.

In the pages ahead, we will look at how you can balance risk to provide both sufficient growth and a sense of security. Certainly, you can expect a reasonable return. You need to keep ahead of inflation, after all, but you should ride the market only with the portion of your portfolio that you can afford to dedicate to that purpose. First you need to make sure that you have saved and invested to create financial independence and that you have identified your goals. Your mission is to stay on course for a successful retirement with a reliable income for the rest of your days. That is why this book is also for younger people and not solely for those nearing retirement age. You need to begin acquiring wealth early and wisely manage your finances over time in a manner appropriate for your age.

Throughout life, financial success has more to do with how much you spend than with how much you make. If you spend more than you make, then you will always feel financially constrained. The discipline of saving regularly, year after year, eliminates the stress of forever wondering how you will get that next hour of pay. Virtually all of my clients have long understood the importance of saving. Some need to do even better, but others have more than enough—and they might not know it. In fact, sometimes the challenge is convincing them that they now can feel confident about their future and can feel free to enjoy their retirement. I encourage them to consider what their money can do for their families or for society at large.

Finding the Game Plan

Each of us has unique dreams and goals. The big question is: what will it take to meet those dreams and goals? No financial plan is the same—at least not the ones that we design. We customize your plan to fit the needs and desires of you and your family. Even so, the patterns are familiar. Rest assured that others have experienced what you are going through. I have seen a wide range of situations, and I have come to recognize the many possible solutions. Some of our most rewarding work has been the planning and ultimate success of seeing our clients overcome adversity, and even despair, to achieve their goals.

I know that sometimes a soul can feel so alone. We can feel as if nobody understands, that nobody has been through what we are going through, whether it's financial adversity, relationship issues, or career struggles. I naively felt that way after I got out of college. It was a stressful time as I tried to figure out where I was going in my career. It wasn't that I was failing as a public accountant, but I was very unhappy. How could I tell my father that I didn't want to be a CPA anymore? How could I let him down?

Things work out with time. Difficult periods in life are important to our personal growth. I know now that I was lucky to have experienced such challenges in my twenties. They prepared me for things to come, and I found, over time, my lifework. Accounting would never have been a good fit for me. I understood the details and appreciated the analytical skills, but my orientation has always been toward the broad view. My passion is to work with people, assisting them in identifying and achieving their goals. I help them find their game plan.

CHAPTER 1

A NEW PERSPECTIVE

*When one door closes, another opens; but we often look
so long and so regretfully upon the closed door that
we do not see the one which has opened for us.*

ALEXANDER GRAHAM BELL

The CPA was crunching the numbers for his own financial future for a change, and what he saw seemed to be good enough. He had not planned to retire just yet—he was losing his job because of a corporate restructuring, but he believed that he had adequate retirement investments. He had nearly $800,000 in savings. His income of $100,000 a year would end, but he was confident that he would become a consultant and that he would bring in at least $50,000 annually and ideally much more.

It didn't work out that way. It had been a long time since he had worked in public accounting, as he had been working primarily for a private employer. He lived in a small town, not a major metropolitan area, which limited his options. Five years into his retirement, he found that he had barely worked as a consultant.

As a result, he was spending more of his assets than he had intended. He had not intended to tap his investments for a while, expecting that they would grow, but he had little choice. While he was withdrawing from his savings, along came the market downturn of 2001. Then 2008 arrived. At that time, he was seventy years old, with no consulting prospects and a vanishing portfolio. He needed more growth from his assets but could not afford to take the risk of downturns because of his high withdrawal rates.

Most people reading this book are no doubt far better positioned, and much of what you will find in the pages ahead is about how to make the most of your wealth. Understand, however, that the experience of that accountant is an all-too-common tale. So many people are hopeful that they can consult to help get them through retirement, or they assume that they will save enough to reach their goals during the last few years that they work. The more likely scenario is that they may be required to accept severance pay from their position earlier than expected and will not find a replacement salary, despite excellent skills. As they get older, even if they could find work, they may begin to feel their energy waning.

This is not how many people envision their retirement. They expect to relax, not to worry about income or desperately look for work. Nonetheless, this is how retirement shapes up for many people who lack a backup plan and did not begin to prepare early enough.

Individuals' goals vary widely as they get closer to retirement. Not everyone wants to retire. In contrast, some do not want to work another day and as a result may retire sooner than they should. Some would have preferred to continue in their careers and have good health and energy. This group is restless in retirement, wishing they could be back at work. Others just felt that so much was changing so fast that they should retire. Perhaps the technology baffled them, or they decided not to invest the time to learn these new skills. Once they leave for good, they feel lost and regret their decision.

A pending retirement requires serious self-reflection. Think about what really brings you joy, and make sure that you are retiring for the right reasons. How will you feel six months after you leave work, realizing that you won't be heading back in? Happiness in retirement is closely correlated with the strength of the personal relationships that you nourish. Men in particular lose many of their relationships when they stop working.

I had a client who ran a small business with ten employees. He began feeling an atmosphere of tension with the staff, and he couldn't pin down the problem. The conflicts were draining him, though, so he finally decided to sell the business and simply retire earlier than he had planned. Later, he learned that it had been one employee who had been generating a lot of the problems. That employee wanted to buy the business and so had been trying to make him uncomfortable. My client eventually started a new business, but he made far less money, and without employees, he had to do it all himself.

The lesson is to be clear about why you are retiring. Take a close look at all the reasons you feel it would be a good idea to leave this career. Are they sufficient to justify ending the work and the relationships that you have built? Don't leave before your time. This may be a permanent move, and it should not be undertaken for transient reasons. When you take this step, it should be toward a goal, not away from an irritant.

Also consider this: When you get to this retirement, how will it feel? What adjustments will be needed on the home front? Many couples have long maintained traditional roles in which the wife was the homemaker and the husband was the breadwinner. They are fine with that. Then the husband retires. The wife, however, does not retire. She still does most of the housework, and she begins to feel frustrated. This is not a case of a lazy husband. Rather, this points to the need to redefine roles during a major transition in life.

This involves more than the division of household duties. For decades, husband and wife have spent only limited hours together each day. Each has maintained, at least to some extent, separate circles of friends and individual interests. He likes to golf, she enjoys her reading club. Are they now expected to spend every waking moment together? They certainly will wish to pursue their dreams as a couple, but each still will need personal time.

I know that these are common issues because I have heard many couples talk about how they feel. We have set up gatherings of clients who are at similar stages, such as pre-retirement, early retirement, or well along the way. Those get-togethers have given them a chance to talk with one another about their experiences. Many have found such open dialogue to be quite helpful.

You simply may not know other people who are going through what you are going through, or if you do, you may not want to be the one to broach these issues. Sometimes it actually is easier to share with people whom you don't know all that well. These gatherings help people to gain much-needed perspectives. How have others handled these matters? Was retirement what they expected? What adjustments did they need to make?

You may feel a sense of loss, for example, when that morning alarm doesn't ring anymore. For many people, a job represents a sizable part of their identity. When the job is no longer there, they feel a sense of emptiness. How will that cup be filled? Many people do not consider that before they retire, and they do not really know how to deal with these feelings. Again, it comes down to learning about yourself and identifying your goals. It is important to find or redefine that personal identity outside of your career.

Personally, I have a spiritual advisor with whom I have spent time talking about personal identity and the workplace. Our work life is but one aspect of who we are, and retirement is an opportunity to grow our physical, mental, and spiritual fitness in many ways. One of my clients said it best: "I thought of retirement as a beginning, not as an end."

A Retirement Tidal Wave

A tidal wave of retiring baby boomers is washing ashore, and that momentum will pick up speed in the years ahead. The United States will have more retirees whose Social Security payments will be supported by fewer workers as the population as a whole ages.

Even for wealthier people, Social Security is a meaningful component of retirement income. If you and your spouse are thinking about retiring on an income of, let's say, $150,000 a year, then the Social Security payments could amount to $30,000 or $40,000 a year for the two of you. This is a significant amount, but it is important to keep in mind that those figures will change. It has happened before, and it may happen again. Each of us needs to look at Social Security as just one component of our retirement income.

For example, all Social Security benefits once were tax-free. Today, depending on the level of income from other sources, up to 85 percent of a couple's benefits may be subject to tax, which can greatly reduce the net amount received. At one time, there was not additional money withheld for Medicare. Today, withholding for Medicare is a significant sum, and it continues to rise.

Retirees should never look at a current benefit and assume that it will continue to sustain them throughout retirement. Benefits are a moving target. Even if the benefit may rise with the cost of living, the government removes portions of it as taxes and medical withholding. I will take a much closer look at Social Security issues later in this book.

Brave New World

Retirement is, in many respects, a brave new world with many new things to consider. These are not the concerns of younger people who are striving to accumulate what they will need for a future that still seems far away. These are the concerns of older people who are ready to start using the assets that they have been accumulating.

Young people tend to think about such things as starting a family, buying a house, saving for the kids' college, and advancing in their careers. They are looking for enough income not only to overcome inflation but also to fulfill their expanding ambitions. They have time on their side, and that time, in itself, is a major asset. They may invest their savings in a manner appropriate to their youth, taking a longer-range view and accepting risks that may be folly when they are close to retirement.

Money that you save when you are in your twenties, properly invested, may grow tenfold by retirement age. Money that you save in your fifties may double by retirement, if you are lucky. Time is no longer on your side at this stage. You have fewer years for your assets to grow or to bounce back from an economic setback. You are reaching the point where the value that you have gained is what you will be living on.

That is why it is so important that retirees move to a mind-set that balances growth with stability. Younger people often invest at relatively higher risk, sometimes putting much of their portfolio at stake. That behavior is not acceptable when you are older, except with a small portion of your money. You wouldn't want to sink your entire nest egg into commodities, for example. You could scuttle your retirement.

In the year 2000, many people guessed that technology stocks were a sure thing and invested heavily in Cisco, Intel, EMC, and others. Index investors who believed that they were well balanced were also at risk because those indexes were so heavily weighted toward tech stocks. Some technology-heavy investors weathered a hit of 80 to 90 percent. This extreme drop in valuations had a lesser effect on upcoming retirees who were invested in more conservative positions.

The lesson, stated simply, is that it is counterproductive to use the same investment strategies in retirement as you did when you were young. You want to take advantage of opportunities, of course, but you need to expose less of your portfolio to those risks. You cannot avoid risk entirely. Your time horizon still is relatively long. If you retire at age sixty-five, there is a reasonable probability that you will live at least twenty more years. For a couple, one or the other spouse is likely to live thirty more years. That is a long time for inflation to perform its mischief. Your portfolio needs to account for inflation but with an appropriate sense of balance.

Even when things don't proceed as you had hoped, you can persevere if you have planned appropriately. If I consulted with a couple, initially when they were in their early fifties, for retirement planning, I would review their life insurance situation. The couple may have had some expensive whole life insurance, yet really not have enough coverage based on the assets they had accumulated. So I may have had them get a term policy with more coverage and advise them to cash in the whole life insurance. In a situation like this, if there were a death of the husband a few years later, with a child in college, this additional coverage would be very important. Having an earlier relationship with a financial advisor before a life-changing event may make a big difference to the surviving partner. In some situations like this, one of the partners may be primarily handling the investments, so the financial advisor relationship may give the surviving partner someone to look to for advice. We may be able to reassure her that their family may be just fine financially. The insurance planning may make the partner financially comfortable after this death.

That is the kind of support that we can offer as people go through such transitions—whether it is something sudden and unforeseen or simply as they venture into what might seem to be the great unknown of retirement.

CHAPTER 2

THE BIG PICTURE

*What we really want to do is what we are really meant to do. When
we do what we are meant to do, money comes to us, doors open
for us, we feel useful, and the work we do feels like play to us.*

JULIA CAMERON

I was never willing to settle for a job. I always took the long-term
view that if I was going to be doing something for forty years,
I had better enjoy it. Successful people become successful
because they have found their perfect niche—something that they
are good at doing and that they genuinely enjoy. Both are necessary.
I have had four distinct careers, and each had elements of a job that
I enjoyed and was challenged by. In accounting I liked tax law; I
was very interested in why laws were in place and what Congress
was seeking to achieve by passing the Roth IRA, for example. I was
in sales for Eastman Kodak. The people part of this—working to
help clients solve their issues with film and the processing of it—was
enjoyable. At Malloy Lithographing, I was hired to put a pricing
system in place. This required understanding the entire manufactur-
ing process and modeling it to effectively price the work. Figuring
out how to price the process of making a book nicely drew on my
analytical side.

Ultimately, financial planning and investment management has been the career that has best drawn on my analytical skills, my interest in people, and my interest in investing. One of the really fun parts about investing is that you need to pull together lots of pieces of disparate information and come to a reasonable conclusion. Is a stock a good buy? You can look at it a hundred different ways, but ultimately you must make a decision. This is also what makes financial planning interesting. Do I have enough to retire? Well, in most cases it depends. How much will you spend? What are your resources? What are the unknowns? That is why I am not an accountant. I have strong analytical skills, but for a fulfilling career I needed more.

I believe that part of my success has been my willingness to accept change and take the career risks of moving on to another job. I was never fired; I always left my jobs seeking something better. In some ways, I was a late bloomer. I did well in school and advanced reasonably in my career, but my business success was certainly not preordained when I was twenty-five, thirty, or even thirty-five. I worked hard, but those early jobs never totally captured my imagination. Ultimately I recognized that those jobs were not what I wished to do for an entire career. Because my wife and I had lived very conservatively, I had the financial flexibility to seek a new career in my late thirties.

We all need to think about what our career will look like. Will you be in a regular job with a stable but modest income, or are you aiming for loftier goals? What is your personality, and what are your skills? Each of us needs to closely evaluate our temperament and talents.

Life is complicated, and we all need to find someone who can look at our situation, identify the specific things we need to do to accomplish our goals, and point out the specific risks we face if we do not take action. I have come to recognize that I have an ability to examine a situation and evaluate it effectively. I have developed these important skills not only during my past careers but also from looking at hundreds of people's situations, doing financial plans for them, and then seeing the results over time. I have adapted as situations change and seen firsthand how different economic periods affect retirement planning.

Throughout this book, I will be using hypothetical situations to illustrate how I may approach the decision making for an individual, family, or business. In all of these situations, my background as a CPA, my graduate education, and my experience in financial advising has framed the next steps for financial guidance. These hypothetical case studies are for illustrative purposes only. Individual cases will vary. Any information is not a complete summary or statement of all available data necessary for making an investment decision and does not constitute a recommendation. Prior to making any investment decision, you should consult with your financial advisor about your individual situation.

The book is written in this format as a result of rules of our industry that prohibit testimonials, as investors may misinterpret it to think this will be the result for them. As a result, all the stories in the book are written as if someone came in with a situation and this is what we would do. This does not alter the fact that we currently serve hundreds of clients and have done planning for virtually all of them. A financial planning office like ours may advise a couple that has made an appointment to review their situation as they are anticipating an inheritance.

In this example situation, Bill and Jean were anticipating an inheritance of $300,000 and as a result were planning to purchase a $600,000 home and two new cars. I believe they may have anticipated our approval and thought that they were well positioned for this spending. I would advise that spending this inheritance would not create the security they desired. In this example, the couple had minimal life insurance. If the husband had died, the wife would have been in a very difficult situation. They were a long way from adequate retirement savings and had not begun saving for their children's college education.

The funds that Bill and Jean were inheriting would put them in a more stable position and give them some liquidity—unless they were lured into buying the more expensive house and expanding their standard of living. This was their critical fork in the road. In situations like this, I would provide more information and choices about how best to preserve the inheritance and about the reality of their current situation. Assuming they adopt this advice and follow a more prudent path, this example might result in this possible outcome:

- They may choose to maximize their annual 401(k) contribution, reducing income taxes and thus probably placing them in a better position for retirement.
- Bill would have a $2 million life insurance policy in place. If he dies, the insurance replaces his income and provides financial security for his family.
- College is now partially funded with money growing tax-free in a 529 plan.
- Bill and Jean would be able to move some of the funds annually into Roth IRAs through what is known as a "backdoor" Roth. (Their situational income would be too high to make a Roth contribution normally.) In ten years,

they may have well over $100,000 growing tax-free in this hypothetical scenario.

- The example family would continue to live in the same home, and because in this situation they have refinanced it with a twenty-year loan, this scenario will result in the home being paid off by the time they retire. The house payments they would pay are calculated to be only slightly more than what they were forecasted to pay on their thirty-year loan.

- The remaining funds (not invested in the Roth or college accounts) may be invested in a tax-efficient manner to avoid generating capital gains or income. If Bill and Jean are charitably inclined, they may use appreciated securities for charitable giving. These rainy-day funds may have the potential to significantly appreciate in value. In contrast, a larger home may or may not increase in value and would have higher annual operating costs, which may have prevented them from accomplishing the savings projection in this scenario.

- One of my recommendations may be a discussion of the advantages of purchasing a two-year-old automobile so the couple would drive the models they preferred and also save money.

The wealth advantages of this planning may become apparent in a decade when Bill and Jean are possibly more comfortable and secure. They may be able to afford to pay for their children's college. If careers are affected by a layoff, they may not be in a crisis, and they may have savings to tap. They may also be in a reasonable retirement situation so that if Bill is not able to replace his job with a similar one, they may still be able to realize some of their retirement dreams.

By taking a more prudent path, this couple has put themselves in a much better position for the future. Inheritances can be watershed events; properly handled, they can really increase financial security.

We are all trying to manage the unknown future. An accomplished financial advisor helps families assess their financial situation and may lead them to the right decisions that may provide stability through upcoming challenges.

You can be certain that challenges do lie ahead, and with the right planning, you can develop the financial reserves to get through struggles without feeling overwhelmed by stress and worry. Living within your means is, again, the solution for attaining that long-term stability. You may need the big-picture perspective to assess whether your lifestyle is in alignment with your goals.

I understand that it is difficult to see that broad view. A comprehensive financial plan includes so many elements that need to align with those forecasted views. Although there are many tools available to help people plan, most of us may benefit from a third party who will look at our situation and assist with evaluating.

Of course, we work with other clients that have required other strategies. The following is an example of how we might handle another retirement challenge.

Tom is a hypothetical client that is planning to retire in a few years. In this example, Tom had accumulated a great deal of wealth in company stock through incentive stock options over the prior decades. His overall total wealth was in excess of $5 million; however, over $3 million of that was in company stock.

Tom had been comfortable with the company stock risk during his working career, but in this scenario, he was no longer comfortable with the risk. Selling the stock and paying capital gains taxes on millions of dollars of capital gains was an unattractive option.

In this situation, a key first part is for us to understand Tom's entire financial picture. We would learn as much as possible about him, his children, and his parents. One angle we would look for is whether there are any gifting strategies, either to parents or children in lower tax brackets for some of the stock. Understanding the whole family is key to this.

Some approaches we would use to help Tom prepare for retirement include:

- One option may be to transfer some shares to children who were in graduate school and not currently employed. Tom could gift over $30,000 to each child, who would sell the stock and pay no taxes because they may be in the 15 percent income tax bracket, where capital gains are taxed at 0 percent. A key part of such gifting is when parents anticipate that their wealth is not just their own but rather as family wealth. In this situation, they may be comfortable gifting. The parents may also need to file a gift tax return, noting that in this situation there may be no tax.

- Another option may be to transfer shares to an exchange fund. Exchange funds take shares of stock and provide an investor with a diversified portfolio not without subjecting you to capital gains on the transfer of the funds. In this example, you have eliminated single-stock risk in exchange for the risk of the overall market. We all have seen once-successful companies fall apart—in some cases even go bankrupt. This is not the kind of risk you want when entering retirement. Only very wealthy investors are able to invest in exchange funds (you need investments of $5 million or more), but they are a great solution for concentrated stock positions.[1]

- Another option may be gifting shares to a donor-advised fund. In this example, Tom was charitably inclined. By gifting some shares in the last year of work, he may reduce taxes in a high-tax year, reducing exposure to company stock, and may build up a fund for future years of possibly more gifting.

In this hypothetical example, Tom reduced his overweight company stock position by over $1 million and avoided paying capital gains taxes on over $750,000 of gains. Tom had an amazing amount of persistent saving, but he needed a way to reduce risk and rebalance his portfolio to generate retirement cash flow. This is the type of advising that I would seek to accomplish for him.

Having a plan in place and working with a knowledgeable advisor can give you confidence that you are moving forward in a productive way. There will always be down periods in the market. When you are still in the accumulation phase, downturns are opportunities to accumulate more assets at lower prices. With a longer-term view, you will look back and see how your wealth accumulated over time and feel confident that you are on the path to reach your goals.

Without a plan, few people reach their goals. It is one thing to say that you want to retire or that you want to retire at age fifty-five.

---

1 Exchange funds are offered as private placements and are not registered under the Investment Company Act of 1940. Therefore, they have strict net-worth requirements that must be met. Your financial advisor should be aware of your investable net worth and other important information before this strategy can be evaluated or recommended. Other considerations you should discuss with your financial advisor include your investment time frame, the liquidity of exchange fund shares, the objectives and actual holdings within a particular fund, and the eligibility of your particular stock. Exchange funds can provide diversification, but please keep in mind that diversification cannot ensure a profit or guarantee against a loss.

It is another thing to build a plan to accomplish this. We see investors not saving enough, putting money in the wrong investments, and not properly diversifying. Those are just a few of the ways that people sabotage their efforts to reach their goals. It makes a difference when you have the support of a professional who is focused on helping you with the big picture.

CHAPTER 3

FINDING THE RIGHT ADVICE

*The most important thing in communication is
hearing what isn't being said. The art of reading
between the lines is a lifelong quest of the wise.*

SHANNON L. ALDER

Most of us understand the principle of collaboration. We use a fitness coach for exercising, and we see a physician for health care. We also often turn to specialists on matters involving our financial lives. The CPA does our tax return, we work with an insurance agent, and we consult with attorneys on an array of legal issues, such as how to best set up an estate. Rarely, however, do those individuals consult with one another. Nobody is pulling it all together.

A financial advisor is the logical person to work with these professionals and gather the required information. Devoting the necessary time is critical. The CPA, attorney, and others typically bill on an hourly basis, so both the client and professional may subconsciously try to keep the time short. You drop off your tax information with the CPA, and that's it for the year; or you meet with an attorney to draw up your will, but you don't see that person again for five or ten years.

You meet your insurance agent when he or she produces your policy, but after that you rarely get together.

Your financial plan is like a voyage, and you need to make course corrections regularly, depending on where you are going in life and the conditions that you encounter. If you were sailing from San Diego to Hawaii, it is unlikely that you would arrive as planned if you did not make navigational adjustments and allowances for wind and current. These corrections ensure that you don't end up in the Cook Islands or somewhere in the South Pacific. A long voyage, like a long life, requires you to track where you are and where you are going.

That is why meeting with our clients at least annually is essential, and in more complicated situations, we meet more frequently. Your financial planner will help you to navigate. These interactions are much more than just a transaction. This is a relationship, and it is very important that you feel comfortable with that person. You need to feel reassurance that he or she takes your best interests to heart and will impart the advice you need to hear, even when it is not what you want to hear.

Anyone earning money could use financial planning advice, although many do not seek it out. Typically, people do not accumulate any real wealth to manage until sometime in their forties or early fifties. Often a visit to an advisor comes about from a job change or an inheritance. I think this is very unfortunate because individuals who do financial planning in their twenties can put themselves in a much stronger situation.

We often give pro bono advice to young people who are just getting started in their careers and need some guidance. It is critical in your twenties to lay the groundwork for the future. My wife and I worked hard to save in our twenties, and that is what gave us the flexibility in our late thirties to have Sabrina focus on our children and to have me launch my financial planning business. Whether financial guidance comes from parents or from a financial advisor, young people need it badly, and frankly, they may be more receptive to listening to the financial advisor.

Getting started early is the key. It takes years to build a portfolio substantial enough to finance retirement, and it also takes time to develop trust and rapport with an advisor who will help guide you.

Although the financial media attracts attention, it is not the best resource for measured, disciplined advice. Much of the financial news is designed to attract attention. Developing a detailed budgeting plan is not very sexy, so it does not command headlines. Steady and consistent savings are the building blocks of financial stability. A good financial advisor knows that. The talking heads on television might know that, but that's not what you will hear about. Their primary aim is to relay stories that grab headlines and increase viewership. These dramatic stories do not necessarily lead to people making sound financial decisions.

I remember all too well working as an advisor in 1999. The media's spotlight was on funds that had returned 100 percent or more for the year and all the technology start-up companies related to the Internet. All the news generated an unparalleled wave of excitement about investing. I had been an advisor for six years at the time, and it was like a faucet had been turned on full blast with all the people who wanted to invest, suddenly conscious that they might miss out if they did not. The public was encouraged by the media to jump in or miss out on a piece of the action. People were determined to invest in this market bubble, but the market was actually nearing the end of an amazing bull run. A much better time to invest would have been 1994, when six years of a bull market were still to come. But the frenzy had not yet built in 1994. By the time people were hyped to invest, it was too late. In fact, fortunes were lost. It was another example of how the media leads people astray.

Keeping You on Track

In our spending society, it is difficult for people to understand how much they can realistically spend and how much they need to save. "We buy things we don't need, with money we don't have, to impress people we don't like."[2] And people often do this by sacrificing funds that they should be setting aside for the future.

One of our goals is to keep you on track and prevent you from making the big mistakes. Most people simply do not look at their situation in a truly comprehensive way. Even when they try, a few oversights combined with some bad luck can turn a good plan into a mess. We all know people who appeared to have successful careers and yet are somehow running out of money during retirement. What went wrong?

The most common problem is that they have overspent and not saved enough. They may have a house that they cannot afford, take elaborate vacations, drive expensive cars, and spend a fortune on their children's private schools and college education without carefully considering price and value. Meanwhile, they save too little. If you are making $250,000 a year and think that saving $18,000 annually in a 401(k) is enough, you should think again. You will need $2 million in investment assets to simply generate $80,000 of income in retirement, unless you are planning to draw down the principal. This assumes a 4 percent withdrawal rate. An income of $80,000 plus Social Security is a long ways from $250,000. In this case I am assuming your portfolio generates a total return of about 6 percent on average over time from

---

2 Quote from Humorist Robert Quillen (1928) and, more recently, Edward Norton in the movie *Fight Club* (1999).

a combination of dividends, interest, and capital appreciation. You spend 4 percent and reinvest 2 percent so that your assets rise and your income over time keeps up with inflation. And what happens if your career is cut short and you are laid off in your fifties? It has happened to many people.

One way we help clients stay on track is through the use of our "Unique Wealth Worksheet." We have presented this at a number of conferences for other advisors, and it has been received with great interest. It allows us and the client to have a really clear understanding of the long-term changes in their overall situation. We have decades of information for some clients here. If you review the following document of hypothetical clients Joe and Sue Smith, you will note the many planning items that come from this. We have just shown two years to make it more readable in the book format.

If you review the following document of hypothetical clients Joe and Sue Smith, you will note the many planning items that come from this. We have shown only three years to make it more readable in the book format. As you look at the Wealth Worksheet on page 37, 38, and 39, note these crucial planning issues:

- How are their liquid savings changing over time?
- Note how their RSU (Restricted Stock Units are shares offered by an employer to an employee in the form of stock) shares are being converted over time into their investment portfolio.
- They have moved a significant amount into a Roth over time for both of them.
- The debt on their home was reduced, and then they paid cash for a new home.
- They have a significant amount in the RJ Charitable Endowment Fund as they near retirement.

- For their son Bob, college may be fully funded or not, depending on their plans. Bob, with the help of his parents, is getting a nice start with a Roth from part-time jobs.
- We have a good snapshot of how much we are carrying in life insurance.
- We see what the tax liability and brackets have been historically, impacted significantly by RSU shares.
- We understand how wage income has changed over time.
- Understanding what has been saved every year is very helpful, and knowing this as a percent of income is also very reinforcing.
- At the bottom of the worksheet, we give a "Measuring up" table to help give clients a sense of where they are in retirement saving. We give a value to the pension since, although it is not an asset per se, it creates an income stream that has a value.

Wealth Tracking Worksheet
Joe and Sue Smith

Joe	01/01/56	60	
Sue	01/01/56	60	

DESCRIPTION	12/31/2013	Percent Change	12/31/2014	Percent Change	12/31/2015	Percent Change
Liquid Investments						
Cash and Cash Equivalents						
Personal Checking and Savings	$ 22,000	-27%	$ 45,000	105%	$ 50,000	11%
Total Cash and Cash Equivalents	$ 22,000	-27%	$ 45,000	105%	$ 50,000	11%
Investments						
Joint Investment Account @ RJ	$ 694,915	0%	$ 894,000	29%	$ 937,000	5%
Joint Bond Account @ RJ	$ 254,720	127%	$ 356,432	40%	$ 372,000	4%
Joe's NQ Stock Options	$ 82,412		$ -		$ -	
Joe's Vested RSUs	$ 336,000		$ 125,000	-63%	$ 325,000	160%
Joe's Unvested RSUs	$ 126,973		$ 225,000	77%	$ 85,000	-62%
Joe's TD Ameritrade Account	$ 117,000		$ 148,690	27%	$ 200,000	35%
Total Investments	$ 1,612,020	29%	$ 1,749,122	9%	$ 1,919,000	10%
Total Liquid Investments	$ 1,634,020	28%	$ 1,794,122	10%	$ 1,969,000	10%
Retirement Investments						
Joe's Retirement Accounts						
IRA @ Raymond James	$ 557,953	14%	$ 577,323	3%	$ 942,834	63%
Tactical IRA @ Raymond James	$ 184,367	31%	$ 205,442	11%	$ 274,047	33%
Roth IRA @ Raymond James	$ 24,000	290%	$ 35,000	46%	$ 188,074	437%
Work 401 K	$ 500,000	43%	$ 587,000	17%	$ -	-100%
Subtotal	$ 1,266,320	28%	$ 1,404,766	11%	$ 1,404,955	0%
Sue's Retirement Accounts						
Roth IRA @ Raymond James	$ 61,669	35%	$ 66,775	8%	$ 73,275	10%
IRA @ Raymond James	$ 140	0%	$ 150	7%	$ 150	0%
Subtotal	$ 61,809	35%	$ 66,925	8%	$ 73,425	10%
Total Retirement Investments	$ 1,328,129	29%	$ 1,471,690	11%	$ 1,478,380	0%
Total Liquid and Retirement Invesments	$ 2,962,148	28%	$ 3,265,812	10%	$ 3,447,380	6%
Total RJ Managed Investments	$ 1,777,763	19%	$ 2,135,122	20%	$ 2,787,380	31%
Homes						
Illinois Home	$ 475,000					
Home Mortgage	$ (225,000)					
Michigan Home			$ 260,000		$ 260,000	
Home Mortgage			$ -		$ -	
	$ 250,000	-21%	$ 260,000	4%	$ 260,000	
Total Homes	$ 250,000	-21%	$ 260,000	4%	$ 260,000	
Unsecured Liabilities						
Credit Card Debt	$ -		$ -		$ -	
Total Unsecured Liabilities	$ -		$ -		$ -	
Net Worth	$ 3,212,148	22%	$ 3,525,812	10%	$ 3,707,380	5%
Change in net worth	$ 584,527		$ 313,664		$ 181,568	
RJ Charitable Endowment Fund	$ 82,483	35%	$ 86,374	5%	$ 81,827	-5%
College Accounts						
MESP Plan FBO Bob Smith	$ -		$ 65,000		$ 72,000	
Bob Smith Roth	$ 16,000	100%	$ 22,773	42%	$ 28,096	23%
Bob Smith 529 Plan	$ 22,351	49%	$ 31,245	40%	$ 37,523	20%
	$ 38,351	67%	$ 119,018	210%	$ 137,619	16%
Life Insurance						
Joe through work	$1,380,000		$1,380,000		$690,000	
Permanent Policy	$100,000		$100,000		$100,000	
Ex work Policy	$170,000		$170,000		$170,000	
	$1,650,000		$1,650,000		$960,000	

Tax Information

AGI	$353,787	$417,074	$111,075
Taxable Income	$294,998	$376,760	$62,325
Federal Tax Liability	$73,834	$99,296	$4,210
AMT	$1,891	$2,351	N
Federal Tax Bracket	35%	35%	15%
State Tax Bracket			
Realized Gain/Loss		$7,500	$4,200
Gain/Loss Used This Year	($3,000)		
Tax Loss Carryforward (at year end)	($51,165)		

Income Sources

Wages			
Joe	$ 230,000	$ 230,000	$ 124,000
Bonus - Usually 20%	$ 46,000	$ 46,000	$ 14,000
Joe- Severance			
Joe - Wages			
Sue	$ -	$ -	$ -
Taxable Account Distributions	$ -	$ -	$ -
Total Income	**$276,000**	**$276,000**	**$138,000**

Account Contributions by Clients

	Taxable Savings			
	RJ Account Saving	$ (1,570)	$ 32,000	$ 24,000
	Gift to DAF			$ (10,031)
H	Retirement Plan Contribution	$ 20,500	$ 20,500	$ -
H	Retirement Plan Contribution	$ 23,712	$ 23,712	$ -
H	Retirement Plan Match- Employer	$ 13,800	$ 13,800	
W	Retirement Plan Contribution	$ -	$ -	$ -
W	Retirement Plan Match- Employer	$ -	$ -	$ -
H	Roth or IRA Contributions	$ -	$ -	$ -
W	Roth or IRA Contributions	$ 6,500	$ 6,500	$ -
	extra payments on mortgage			
	Total Saved	**$62,942**	**$96,512**	**$13,969**

Roth Contribution for the Year

Joe			
Sue	$6,500	$6,500	0

Tracking Ratios

Total Investments	$ 2,962,148	$ 3,265,812	$ 3,447,380
Investments to Income	10.7	11.8	25.0
Value of Pension	$1,000,000	$1,000,000	$1,000,000
Investments to Income with pension	14.36	15.46	32.23
Total Debt	$ (85,000)	$ -	$ -
Debt to Income	0.3	0.0	0.0
Annual Savings as a Percent of Income	22.8%	35.0%	10.1%

Measuring Up			
Are your finances on track? Look Below. If you're age 50 and earn $100,000, you should have at least $640,000 in Investments and < $75,000 of debt.			
	Investments-to-Income		Debt-to-
Age	$100,000	$175,000	$250,000	Income
30	3.6	3.8	3.8	1.70
35	4.4	4.7	4.7	1.50
40	5.1	5.8	5.8	1.25
45	5.9	7.2	7.2	1.00
50	6.4	8.6	8.9	0.75
55	6.7	10.3	11.0	0.50
60	8.3	12.0	13.7	0.20
65	9.9	14.2	16.2	0.00

The accompanying Wealth Tracking Worksheet was prepared solely to help you track progress on your personal financial plan. Accordingly, it may be incomplete or contain other departures from generally accepted accounting principles and should not be used to obtain credit or for any other purposes other than developing your financial plan. We have not audited, reviewed or compiled the statement.

This report is not a replacement for the official customer account statements from Raymond James or other custodians. Investors are reminded to compare the findings in this report to their official customer account statements. In the event of a discrepancy, the custodian's valuation shall prevail. This data is furnished to you as a courtesy and for informational purposes only. This report may include assets that the firm does not hold on your behalf and which are not included on the firm's books and records. Although this data is derived from information which we believe to be accurate (including, in some cases information provided to us by you) we cannot guarantee its accuracy. This information is not intended and should not be used for any official tax, lending, legal, or other non-financial planning purposes and should not be relied upon by third parties. Performance data quoted represents past performance and does not guarantee future results. The investment return and principal of an investment will fluctuate so that an investor's shares when redeemed may be worth more or less than the original cost. The values represented in this report may not reflect the true original cost of the client's initial investment. Please contact your financial representative if there has been a change in your investment objectives, special restrictions, or financial circumstances.

Raymond James Financial Services, Inc.
Member FINRA/SIPC
Douglas B. Gross, CFP®, Financial Advisor
315 E. Eisenhower Blvd. Suite 301
Ann Arbor, MI 48108
Phone 734.944.7556

Another serious problem is a lack of sufficient life insurance. Life insurance protects the spouse who has a more modest job or who is a homemaker in the event that the primary wage earner dies prematurely. Too few families recognize the need for more life insurance as a career accelerates and obligations like children, housing, and lifestyle run ahead of savings. If a family's income increases significantly and then one of the wage earners dies, the family needs much greater assets to continue that lifestyle. It takes a long time to build such a base of wealth. Therefore, the family needs much more life insurance to cover that gap.

Poor investment management also contributes to insufficient funds. Key issues we see are investors sitting on way too much cash and being poorly diversified. In recent years, that situation has markedly improved with the advent of "lifestyle" and "target-date" investments that provide much more diversification and automatic rebalancing. However, the risk of overconcentration remains, particularly for people with a portfolio that is overweight in company stock or some other position. Also, investors rarely update their portfolio allocation by rebalancing, partly because they are uncertain of the nature of those investments. A competent advisor can play an essential role in adding value by rebalancing and making sure the investments are allocated for tax efficiency.

In Your Best Interests

How do you choose a qualified advisor you can trust to act in your best interest? I think it is difficult. The good news is that there are many advisors that are client focused. When choosing an advisor, see whether they are asking questions with the goal of doing effective planning or if they are more focused on gathering your assets that they wish to be paid to invest. Of course, advisors will tell you that the way they operate is the best way for you. You will hear from fee-only advisors, for example, that they are the only ones who are truly looking out for your best interest. In reality, they may want to put their clients' assets into accounts that will pay fees, which may or may not make sense depending upon the situation.

Our practice is generally fee-based, but we also recognize that you really should not pay a fee on some assets. As an example, consider a thirty-year municipal bond that yields 4 percent. If your advisor charges you 1 percent to hold that bond, then a quarter of your return per year goes to the advisor. We do buy municipal bond funds, and people do pay us fees on those. For larger accounts, however, we generally try to buy individual municipal bonds and hold them to maturity. The fee on that municipal bond is a one-time commission. Some in the industry consider commissions to be almost a dirty word, but in this case, the cost to the client might be 2 percent to buy that bond—and that is much less than the long-term cost of paying an annual fee over thirty years. A fee of even .50 percent over thirty years adds up to 15 percent, far more than a 2 percent commission. The way your advisor should be operating is to position your assets in the most reasonable manner while looking for ways to manage your costs. There has been much discussion regarding passive versus active investments and what the right investment vehicles are. You might be led to believe that there is just one answer, but that is simply not the case. Once again, the situation governs the decision, and you need someone to advise you about the best strategies for your specific needs.

As CERTIFIED FINANCIAL PLANNERS™, we recognize our role as fiduciaries: to always act in the client's best interest. The federal government has been pushing to tighten fiduciary regulations, and various parts of the industry have been fighting that. Many advisors who are not fiduciaries instead are held to a suitability standard. If the investment is deemed to be suitable for a situation, then that is sufficient.

Nonetheless, advisors who stand on a soapbox and say they are fiduciaries yet charge high fees may not be truly acting as fiduciaries. It is always important for investors to understand the total cost of their investments and for advisors to fully disclose their fees.

Finding a Good Advisor

How do you identify a good advisor? You can start with referrals. Talk to CPAs, attorneys, and your friends to get a sense of whom they are working with and what they like about those advisors. You can also go to an advisor's seminar to learn more about him or her, but the best marketers are not necessarily the best advisors. Many of the best advisors do very little marketing; instead, their business has grown organically through referrals.

Sometimes people come in to see us, and their main objective is to hire an advisor who can beat the market every year and make big money for them. Some advisors will put together a portfolio and boast about how it performed over the previous five years. If you look more closely, you very likely will find that the advisor did not have that portfolio five years earlier. The reality is that the advisor has put together a collection of investments that, in hindsight, have done well and is simply suggesting to clients that they should follow suit. It amounts to chasing performance. It doesn't work that way. Historically, chasing performance results in an underperforming portfolio. And so the client, disappointed by the results, moves on to another advisor.

If you look at the data, it is clear that even the great investors of all kinds have periods of one to three years when they have underperformed, for whatever reason—perhaps their style is out of favor. They have other periods where they outperform the average. Investors ultimately achieve success when they have the patience to work through those periods of underperformance. Those who chase performance and move from investment to investment or advisor to advisor may not be recognizing the real problem: themselves. This is not to say you should never fire an advisor, but just be sure that you are moving on for the right reasons.

How can you tell whether you're getting the service you need? If your meetings with the advisor feel more like a social event or an opportunity for your advisor to pontificate about the markets, you are probably not getting what you need. Real planning takes time. Your advisor needs to ask you for a lot of information and then use it to give you feedback. Has the advisor asked for a copy of your tax return and your 401(k) statements? Have beneficiary elections been reviewed to make sure they are current? Those are just a few of the considerations that need to be addressed. This advance preparation is a foundation to build on and adds value to the relationship.

Here are some red flags indicating that you may have the wrong advisor:

- Your IRA investments look the same as your taxable investments. One reason that they should look different is because they are taxed differently. In an IRA, gains are only taxed on withdrawal. Many investments are very tax inefficient and simply are poor investments in a taxable account, spinning out gains, sometimes even in years when they lose money. Your time horizons for withdrawals may also differ between taxable and tax-deferred accounts, so you may wish to invest in them at different levels of risk.

- Your advisor is not planning how you can minimize your taxes in retirement and is not forecasting your tax liability through your midseventies. Retirement can be an opportunity to finally get a break from those high-tax years. If properly designed, the portfolio may allow you to be in the 15 percent bracket in your early retirement years and reduce taxes, significantly helping with cash flow. To best achieve this, you need to build up your tax-free Roth and after-tax assets during your working years. In many cases you can then tap those assets in retirement with little tax impact.

- If your advisor is more focused on the product they are providing than on planning your future, be cautious. Typically this kind of advisor is talking about high yields and high returns and is probably not disclosing fees. I would be cautious any time there is a one-size-fits-all solution. Whenever anyone tells me something does not have a cost, I am very wary.

- Your advisor seems reluctant to explain how he or she is paid and to give you a total figure. You need to know that amount so that you can possibly deduct it on your tax return.

In selecting an advisor, try to get a feel for his or her thirst for education. The investment and planning fields are changing constantly. Is the advisor a CERTIFIED FINANCIAL PLANNERS™? Has he or she pursued a master's degree? Ask for examples of the financial planning process and how it would help you in your situation. Will the advisor be managing your portfolio, or will it be managed by a third party? If it's a third party, what are the costs and fees involved with this organization? Investors should seek to understand their total investment costs. Advisors' total fees in excess of 1 percent are on the high side, and the percent charged for investors with $2 to 3 million in assets should be well under 1 percent unless services offered are very extensive. Investors with fewer assets may face slightly higher fees.

Find out how the staff will assist you and who you should contact for what services. Many advisors simply do not have the trained staff to appropriately address issues and be of assistance. A trained staff with many years of experience is able to handle calculating cost basis, transferring funds, opening accounts, and numerous other issues to make your financial life easier.

A Foundation of Trust

For more than twenty years, I have worked with another sort of advisor: a spiritual advisor. Early in my career, when I was in my late thirties, he suggested that I should be mentally prepared for the day that surely would come when my clients were losing money. I told him at the time that I did not see that happening; I was working really hard at being a good advisor and would pick good investments for people. They could trust me, I assured him, to do well by them.

I had no idea how correct he was. I am confident that we have done a good job of advising and managing assets for clients, but I also was with them through the two horrendous bear markets in the first decade of the millennium. I have learned a lot about managing expectations and helping people build portfolios that endure the down times. I understand the damage that results when investors bail out at the bottom and do not get back in.

Through good times and bad, investors need professional guidance and a strong relationship with their advisor. I saw the strength of those relationships during 2008–09. Although clients clearly were unhappy about the losses, they also expressed sincere concerns about how my colleagues and I were dealing with the stress. That is the caliber of the people we have been fortunate enough to serve. They are as concerned about us as we are about them.

Investors need to remain passionately dispassionate about the markets. The more emotionally charged you get about investing, the less success you are likely to find. We care deeply about the decisions we make on our clients' behalf, but we try to keep the emotions out of the investing. When you start thinking you're a genius, that's when you are likely to get clobbered with an unforeseen loss. Investing is a humbling business.

Trust is the key. A 2015 worldwide survey published in *The Wall Street Journal* found that people are happiest in countries where they have money, good health, and feel they can trust one another.[3] The happiest country turned out to be Switzerland, where honesty seems to be a way of life and is expected in all transactions. It is a model for all of us. Trust is what builds solid relationships, through good times and bad. When you find a financial advisor who truly keeps your best interest in mind and will be there for you and your family for the long term, you are laying the foundation for your success.

3 Jo Craven McGinty, "On Gauging the Pursuit of Happiness," *The Wall Street Journal*, August 21, 2015, http://www.wsj.com/articles/on-gauging-the-pursuit-of-happiness-1440149401.

CHAPTER 4

WEIGHING THE RISKS

*In all affairs, it's a healthy thing now and then to hang a
question mark on the things you have long taken for granted.*

BERTRAND RUSSELL

Wealthy people typically have attained their status by in
some way accumulating wealth, almost always over
longer periods of time. Inherited wealth is actually
surprisingly not the source of most wealth today, with less than 20
percent of the wealthy having inherited the funds. In many cases,
people's wealth was created by starting a successful company in which
they have significant equity or by rising through the ranks of an organization and acquiring valuable stock options. Wealth is also created
by simply saving on a consistent basis over many years. Regardless of
how wealth is created, people are at great risk of losing much of what
they have gained without adequate foresight.

Business owners often have much of their net worth tied up in
their company. The same is true for successful employees who have
received equity in their company. Over time, the company stock
typically becomes their number-one investment position. In either
case, these are people who have what we call "single-stock risk." A
great deal is riding on how well the company does.

It's generally true that the best investment that business owners will ever make is in their own company. By controlling that asset, they can leverage it with more sales and may grow its value by 20 or 30 percent a year or more. However, the value of that company also may drop significantly over time, and that is why business owners must develop outside assets. I have seen cases where people have worked hard for decades just to see their business lose most of its value for one reason or another. They were on the verge of retirement, and then they had nothing to retire on.

There are many ways for business owners to create those critical nonbusiness assets. One easy way is to start a 401(k) or other retirement plan. They should also build up personal savings and investments outside the business that will provide them with liquidity. That way, they can sustain the business during hard times and will have access to money that is not tied up in their operations.

Without diversity, market investors face similar risk. They may have a holding that does exceedingly well and claims a greater and greater portion of the portfolio. Then comes a time when that investment no longer works out.

For example, local banks historically have been a nice investment, with steady dividends and reasonable growth. In addition, the investors tend to know the people running the business. They get comfortable with these companies, and if the local bank pays a cash dividend and perhaps some stock dividends, annual returns could be significant without the stock increasing in value.

Here in southeast Michigan, many investors watched their wealth grow nicely by owning shares at United Bank and Trust. Not many shares were available to investors, so the stock had limited volatility and consistently rose in price as demand for shares exceeded supply. It was a very well-run bank. Even in market downturns, the stock was remarkably stable.

The bank gradually grew from a small community bank to a regional player, establishing itself in Ann Arbor, a rapidly growing city. For over a decade, investors were well rewarded and became comfortable, with a significant portion of their wealth invested in the bank. They felt encouraged by how nicely the bank weathered the 2001–03 market downturn.

Unfortunately, the bank's efforts to grow led it to make a large number of real estate loans. They were an important part of that growth, and they peaked just before the financial crisis of 2008–09. Many of those loans defaulted. The bank's earnings collapsed, and the bad real estate loans piled up on the books. The bank accepted an outside investor who injected capital at around $2.50 a share, a long way from the $30 and $40 range where it once traded. Dividends were also suspended. Many investors who counted on the dividends for income both no longer had the income and had seen the value of their holding plummet.[4]

Compounding the problem, the limited float of the stock now made it hard to sell without a drop of at least ten to fifteen cents a share, sometimes quite a bit more. Investors who waited it out recovered some of their losses; the bank was sold a few years later to another bank for about $12 a share. For those who had been investing for fifteen years, the investment ultimately was profitable. The risk-takers who jumped in at $2.50 were well rewarded, gaining five times their money in just a few years. Although some benefited, it was by no means a sure thing, and it could have been worse. Many

---

4 David Frownfelder, "UB&T, Old National Bank announce Merger," Lencon-nect.com, January 8, 2014, http://www.lenconnect.com/article/20140108/BUSINESS/140109353.

banks went bankrupt in 2008–09. Investors with highly concentrated positions in the bank suffered a dramatic reduction in their wealth.[5]

Such is the risk of a concentrated position, even when you know that there are good people running the bank who have been doing an adequate job. They can make mistakes. Economic changes can devastate even the best companies. Think about all those technology companies in the 1990s that were thought to be the future and instead vanished.

What can investors do? Certainly, the lesson here is to manage your single-stock risk. If you're getting stock options or restricted stock from your employer, it's critical that you do not allow this stock position to get out of line with the rest of your portfolio. Investors need to think hard about how they might diversify out of a stock when it exceeds 20 to 25 percent of their portfolio.

If you are a company insider and the sale of your stock is restricted, you could pursue a few different strategies. Generally, you will have certain periods of the year, or windows, in which you will be allowed to sell, so you may take advantage of those. Also, you may sign an agreement for systematic sales, selling the stock regularly and consistently. You would lose the ability to time the sales, but at least you would be reducing the size of your position and reducing your risk.

Here's another story about the risk of concentrated stock positions. The 1990s were an amazing period for drug discovery, and pharmaceutical stocks rocketed up. In 2000, Pfizer bought Warner-Lambert, whose employees in Ann Arbor became Pfizer employees.[6] Warner stock had lagged for much of the 1980s and 1990s, and the

---

5 "United Bancorp Inc.: Form 424B1," EdgarOnline, prospectus, December 14, 2010.

6 Martha Slud, "Pfizer, W-L strike deal", CNN Money, August 30, 2016, http://money.cnn.com/2000/02/07/deals/warner_lambert/.

acquisition by Pfizer worked out very well for employees who had received stock options.[7]

Imagine a scenario in which you worked for Warner and had stock options that you could exercise for between $15 and $20 a share. Pfizer then comes in and converts your options into Pfizer options.[8] Pfizer was soon to bring the record-selling Lipitor to market (the drug had been developed at Warner-Lambert), and its stock topped $50 a share.[9] That meant that a Warner-Lambert employee who had ten thousand options might have gained $30 a share or $300,000 before taxes.

About the same time, Pfizer was introducing Viagra, and sales were soaring.[10] Pfizer employees understandably might have wondered why they would ever exercise and sell their shares. The future looked very bright indeed. In hindsight, it may have been the time to sell. The pharmaceutical industry was about to slow down as fewer products hit the market and other drugs came off their patents.[11] The only way many companies were growing earnings was through acquisitions.[12] Pfizer ultimately bought Upjohn and Wyeth.

---

7 Joseph Weber, "Offering Employees Stock Options They Can't Refuse", Bloomberg, October 7, 1991, http://www.bloomberg.com/news/articles/1991-10-06/offering-employees-stock-options-they-cant-refuse.

8 "Legacy Warner-Lambert Equity Compensation Plans," excerpt taken from the *PFE DEF 14A* filed March 13, 2009, http://www.wikinvest.com/stock/Pfizer_(PFE)/Legacy_Warner-lambert_Equity_Compensation_Plans.

9 Christopher Bowe, "Say Farewell to Lipitor but Don't Forget Its Lessons," *Harvard Business Review*, August 18, 2011, https://hbr.org/2011/11/say-farewell-to-lipitor-but-do.

10 Martha Slud, "Pfizer, W-L strike deal."

11 Mark Gimein, Louis Lavelle, Amy Barrett, Dean Foust, and bureau reports, "The Bottom Line on Options," Bloomberg, April 2, 2006, http://www.bloomberg.com/news/articles/2006-04-02/the-bottom-line-on-options.

12 Laura Brodbeck, "The 15 Biggest Mergers of All Time", Yahoo Finance, October 19, 2015, http://finance.yahoo.com/news/15-biggest-mergers-time-175152979.html.

The stock however had peaked in 2000 and began a gradual decline down to $12 a share by 2009.[13]

If you were an employee hired in 2000 and got stock options at $50 a share, they would have expired as essentially worthless because the stock never rose above that range over the next seven years.[14] You would have been much better off had you been hired by Warner-Lambert back in the 1980s or 1990s and eligible for options when the company wasn't performing as well.

It's another example of why investors need to take some money off the table, even when expectations are high and even when it would mean paying a tax bill. Some investors who had an opportunity for a huge windfall ended up with nothing. Stock options are a leveraged investment. Your risk lies in the spread between your exercise price and the market price. It is critical that you successfully manage that risk, as well as the risk of having too much of your wealth tied up in a single stock.

Other Investment Risks

What I have been describing is *market risk*—and market risk is just one example of the variety of threats to your portfolio that can become increasingly troublesome as you approach retirement. Most investors, when they hear the word risk, think first of the stock market, and that indeed is where so many people lost so much in the 2008–09 downturns, with many of them missing the recovery as well.

It is a risk that can affect you very differently depending upon your stage in life. For young people still building wealth, the 2008–09 crash was, in many ways, a tremendous investment opportunity.

13 NYSE Historical Prices database 1/1/2000 – 12/31/2009: Pfizer, Inc. PFE
14 NYSE Historical Prices database 1/1/2000 – 12/31/2010: Pfizer, Inc. PFE

They could buy shares at a bargain price, getting perhaps twice as many shares for the same money as they would have before the crash. Investors who put money in regularly were actually well ahead within two or three years of the market drop. However, retirees who were withdrawing money when the market plunged did not fare so well. If they were fully exposed to that risk, it often was next to impossible to recover, even with a healthy rebound in the market.

That's a key reason that retirees need a more conservative portfolio. Your risks are different when you're withdrawing money than when you're investing money. And when the market drops, you cannot decide abruptly to become more conservative. Retirees need their portfolios positioned with a level of risk they can live with through a downturn. Those who dramatically reduce risk during a downturn will be locking in those losses without hope for any rebound. You will get all the downside but none of the upside. We help our clients visualize just what could happen with a program called Riskalyze, which projects potential losses based on their current portfolio in a market crisis. It helps them decide whether their current portfolio situation is a risk they would be willing to take.

It is also important to regularly monitor your portfolio to decide whether the asset allocation should be rebalanced. The goal is to periodically sell some of the winners to put more money into investments that are inexpensive. Let's say you were Rip Van Winkle and went to sleep in 1980 with your portfolio split 50/50 between stocks and bonds. When you woke up in 2000, you would have found that you had about 75 percent in stocks and 25 percent in bonds. You didn't change the percentages—it was a natural result of the winners claiming a progressively larger share of this neglected portfolio.

Using the following Riskalyze chart, clients can quickly understand what the risk has been historically with their portfolio allocations.

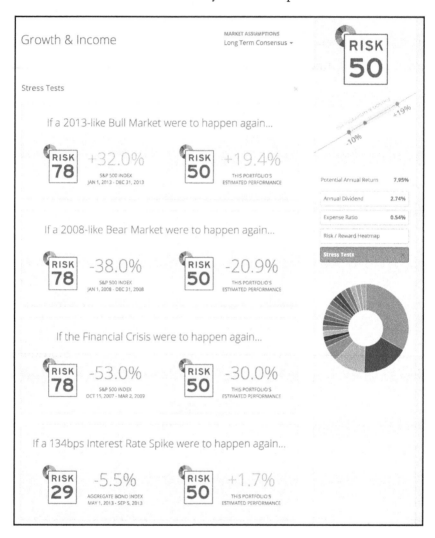

By regularly managing and adjusting your allocation, you avoid your portfolio becoming increasingly risky over time—particularly when you are about to retire and probably want to invest more conservatively. It feels counterintuitive, but you may need to take some money away from the winners and move it to the losers.

That was the situation before the dot-com bust. By 2000, technology stocks had grown and grown to become 40 percent of the market. Many investors weren't willing to sell those stocks, because their future looked so bright. Meanwhile, value stocks were out of favor and very inexpensive. If investors had simply moved to value stocks, the coming crash would not have damaged their investments so significantly. Many, however, failed to rebalance their portfolio—and the market rebalanced it for them.

Retirees need to be aware of what is known as sequence of return risk. Ideally you will retire in a period when the market is rising and continues to rise; then, if it drops in later years, you won't feel as much of an impact. In contrast, if you retire in a year like 2007 and the market drops in the early years, you may never recover. It is essential to structure your portfolio properly as you enter retirement, carefully considering how much money you will be withdrawing and positioning yourself so that if returns are poor in the early years of your retirement, your portfolio remains intact.[15]

The Risk of Market Timing

Quite frankly, what has sunk many a portfolio is the human propensity to sell at the bottom of the market, getting the timing entirely wrong. Historically, investors have bought what's hot, getting in at the peak and, disappointed at the decline, bailing out after taking a beating. To do the opposite takes discipline, which is in short supply among amateur investors.

Peter Lynch, who was once a well-known mutual fund manager, once pointed out that many individual investors often lose money in investments that are ultimately profitable over the long term. The

---

15 Diversification and asset allocation do not ensure a profit of guarantee against a loss.

truth of that assertion has been documented. How is that possible? Because all-too-eager investors would often wait until a particular investment had two or three good years and would then decide that it was high time to jump in. Then the market would turn down, and they would suffer losses. "Forget it, I'm out of here," they would say, selling before the next upward cycle. Instead, that was a time when they should have been doubling down on the investment.

As I have mentioned, growth-oriented investors think of dips in the market as opportunities. Investors who have a reserve of both bonds and cash have the liquidity to take advantage of those opportunities and to protect themselves in downturns. If you have built up wealth over time and you have money available, then when the stock market drops, you're able to invest and take advantage of it. If you lack available conservative investments, you may miss opportunities to create real wealth.

Even when they can, many investors don't put money to work in downturns. They may know intuitively what they should do, but often they fail to take action. It doesn't come naturally to bid farewell to what seems to be a good thing and to buy into what seems to be a loser. That, however, is what makes money. People fall victim to greed and fear. In the end, the greatest risk can be our emotions.

Inflation Risk

Aside from market risk, the threat of inflation is significant. Many people remember the double-digit inflation days of the 1970s and 1980s. There is the risk that the cost of living may rise faster than your income grows, effectively shrinking your standard of living. Investors in countries like Venezuela today are watching inflation devastate the value of their holdings. For this reason, many investors in countries with high inflation or less stable currencies park a significant portion of their wealth in the United States, Switzerland, or other countries that have historically been much more stable.

After three decades of declining interest rates, investors are not expecting a significant rise in interest rates. But one can never be certain, and that risk clearly has been present in several parts of the world recently. For investors anywhere, however, inflation cannot be discounted. It is a very real threat to your financial well-being.

Inflation takes its toll slowly, eroding a portfolio over the years, and it is especially troubling to retirees on fixed pensions. Health-care costs' inflation is particularly insidious, as health care is generally a growing portion of your spending as a retiree. If you retire at age sixty-five with an income of $4,000 a month, by the time you are eighty-five, inflation and growing health-care costs may have reduced your purchasing power by 30 to 50 percent. You will need growing assets to provide a rising income to make up that difference.

Interest Rate Risk

Investors in bonds face risks both from rising and falling interest rates. If you recall the days when certificates of deposit (CDs) or money markets could yield 5 or 6 percent or more, you can understand the concept of interest rate risk. If you had $1 million in those investments, you were earning $50,000 to $60,000 a year, and you may have felt pretty comfortable. Well, today CDs pay 1 percent, and the reality is that you're effectively not getting paid anything on your cash. Most money markets today have a yield of zero or a fraction above that. After inflation, investors are losing money. Investors that kept their bond money in very short-term investments have really suffered, with declining interest rates devastating their incomes.

Rising interest rates are a particularly acute risk for bond investors. As interest rates rise, the value of bonds falls. What is an investor to do? You cannot keep all of your money in short-term investments. It is important that investors build out bond ladders to lock in interest rates on a longer-term basis or simply diversify themselves into bond funds containing bonds with different maturities.

One strategy is to buy individual municipal bonds. You can buy individual bonds with terms of five, ten, fifteen, twenty, or thirty years. By doing that, you can lock in your yield on the overall portfolio for quite some period of time. You will have to periodically reinvest as your shorter-term bonds mature, but you can lock in your income for a time and protect yourself from interest rates going down. If interest rates go up, you may think it would be devastating—but you always will have some bonds maturing, and you simply buy more bonds further out. Over time, in a flat-yield environment, your yield rises as you replace maturing bonds with longer-term bonds.

For your fixed-income investments, your overall return over ten years will almost always look much like the yield of the portfolio at the start of the period, assuming you have investments with medium to longer maturities. So if you buy a portfolio of bonds yielding 3 or 4 percent, your returns over ten years should be in that 3 to 4 percent range.[16] CD investors, on the other hand, who bought short-term CDs quickly, saw their yield and total returns drop as interest rates fell. A balanced portfolio of different types of bonds with varying maturities provides a much more stable income over the long term than short-term CDs.

---

16 CDs are insured by the Federal Deposit Insurance Corporation (FDIC) and offer a fixed rate of return, whereas the return and principal value of investment securities fluctuate with changes in market conditions.

The Risk of Fraud

If you watch the television show *American Greed*, you may conclude that there is a charlatan on every corner, poised to take your money. There certainly are some out there, but a few simple precautions can significantly reduce the likelihood that someone will take advantage of you.

The most common risk, in my observation, is investing privately in a company or handing over management of your assets to someone who does not hold them at a known brokerage firm. Here are a few examples of these types of investment:

- Simon, your neighbor, tells you about a friend whose firm is developing a unique drug. They are nearing the last stages of development, but they need additional investors. Banks won't lend to them (because they have no assets), so they are seeking private funding. Venture capital won't touch them; they cannot really make a viable case, or perhaps they are too small.

  This is where you come in. You give them $50,000 and now own 5 percent of the company. Chances are you will never see that money again. You have shares of a privately held company, and even if the company is ultimately successful, you will be hard-pressed to get your money back or to participate in the success. Unless they take the company public, you don't have an easy way to force them to share profits with you or to refund your money. Sometimes the business simply disappears, and there is nothing to pay you back.

This is not to say that private investments never work out, but investors need to be very cautious and never invest money in schemes like this unless they can afford to lose the money.

- When people invested with Bernie Madoff, they did not make out a check to Charles Schwab, Merrill Lynch, or Raymond James. They made out checks to Bernard Madoff Investment Securities, LLC. When you do something like that, do you wonder whether you are getting the standard protections of a major brokerage firm? The Securities Investor Protection Corporation (SIPC) restores investors' cash and securities up to certain limits if the firm should financially collapse.[17] Investors are protected if a broker at a major firm should steal their money. If this unlikely event occurs, the brokerage would step in and make you whole up to certain limits. When Bernie Madoff stole money from investors, leading to the collapse of his firm, there was no one to step in. Investors have made some recovery, but the losses remain staggering.

What should you watch for? One obviously suspicious sign are claims such as "We have never lost our investors' money!" or "We guarantee 8 percent or more as returns annually!" Also, be wary if you are asked to

---

17 The Securities Investor Protection Corporation (SIPC) protects against the loss of cash and securities—such as stocks and bonds—held by a customer at a financially troubled SIPC-member brokerage rm. The limit of SIPC protection is $500,000, which includes a $250,000 limit for cash. An explanatory brochure is available upon request at SIPC.org or by calling (202) 371-8300.

just write out a check to an individual rather than to a bank or investment firm.

- We periodically have clients whose e-mail accounts have been hacked. We might get an urgent request via e-mail to send money to an offshore bank. We always immediately contact the client and never send funds to outside accounts based on an e-mail request. Your financial services provider should act in the same manner.

Other Threats to Your Wealth

In the chapters ahead, we will look at other significant risks to your wealth. We will examine the toll of taxation, for example, and strategies to reduce how much you must pay. We will look at the risk that you or your spouse will need long-term care, which can be devastating to your finances.

Certainly, a divorce or the death of a spouse can have a huge impact on people's lives. Never hesitate to seek out counseling to maintain the health of your marriage. And take good care of yourself. Do your best to keep yourself in shape to enjoy a long retirement.

It is important that both spouses understand the portfolio and what they are seeking to accomplish as a couple. Quite often I see that one spouse or the other has little understanding or interest in their investments. We believe it is critical that both spouses attend meetings with a financial advisor and develop a working relationship with the advisor. If one spouse should die, the survivor needs to feel confident in the advisor who will be looking out for his or her financial welfare. In the case of a divorce, if it comes to that, a trusted advisor can help both partners figure out the best path.

Ironically, you will need to consider the risk that you might live a long time. The whole point of pension plans was to eliminate longevity risk. The pension continues to pay income until the time of death. Assuming pensioners elect joint and survivor benefits, the benefits continue over the lives of both spouses. Today, longevity risk has become a far more serious threat. Most of us do not have pensions. When you are drawing down assets from your own investments and the market suddenly turns sharply south, your nest egg may dwindle to the point where you run out of money.

The difference between having half a million dollars and running out of money may be a matter of ten years or less. You can circumvent longevity risk by spending less, postponing expenses, or finding a way to earn more income. Occasionally we buy a single-premium immediate annuity for clients to produce a lifetime of pension-like income. It is an important option for those who feel the threat on the horizon that they will run out of money. You certainly don't want to get into that position, but it is a real risk for people who are drawing down assets.

Investors who have a financial plan and regularly monitor their portfolios and update their plan have a much higher chance of success than investors who do not plan. Risks are always changing, and the investor who takes the time to stay on top of their situation is the one who can most successfully minimize risk.

> Every investor's situation is unique, and you should consider your investment goals, risk tolerance, and time horizon before making any investment. Investing involves risk, and you may incur a profit or loss. Keep in mind that there is no assurance that any strategy will ultimately be successful or profitable against a loss.

CHAPTER 5

ATTENDING TO TAXES

*. . . but in this world, nothing can be said to
be certain, except death and taxes.*

BENJAMIN FRANKLIN

O ne of the greatest challenges to the accumulation of
wealth is taxes. Most people spend what is left from their
paycheck after withholding for taxes and retirement
savings every month. As a result, most wealth is accumulated in tax-
deferred savings plans, and after-tax wealth that might be used to
build businesses or invest is typically very modest until people reach
the upper income levels.

A few years ago, I had the opportunity to spend some time in
Paraguay and chatted with residents there about their accumulation
of wealth. In Paraguay, even the wealthy pay little or no personal
income taxes. The money that they make is theirs, and people are
able to accumulate wealth quickly. There are, of course, trade-offs: the
public infrastructure and social safety net are very different compared
to those in the United States. Although Paraguay is attractive from a
wealth-building standpoint, a lack of such a safety net would be quite
problematic in a country like ours.

In contrast, in the United States, once your family's taxable earnings pass $75,000, you will pay federal taxes at a marginal rate of 25 percent of your income. As your income climbs to over $460,000, the marginal tax rate increases to 39 percent, and total taxes could exceed 50 percent or more if you include sales, property, and state taxes. Many make the mistake of believing that if they are making half a million dollars a year, they should be able to buy and spend freely, and they act as though they can. They are not taking into account the impact of taxes.

Investors must always be conscious of the effect of taxes on their wealth accumulation and do what they can to minimize those taxes. Until the 1980s, the common strategy of the wealthy was to invest in oil, gas, and other partnerships that offered tax preferences to reduce taxes. However, the government has gradually eliminated most of those tax breaks, and for many, the alternative minimum tax has had a significant impact. As a result, investors need to seek to invest in a more tax-efficient way. Buying an investment with tax preferences to reduce your taxes after the fact is generally no longer a viable strategy.

Tax-Efficient Portfolio Structure

Investors should strive to manage their portfolio in a tax-efficient manner. For example, in the first decade of the millennium and as a result of two significant market slumps, many investments did not generate large taxable distributions. This is because the investments may have built up losses during the market slumps. Some types of investments are required to distribute 95 percent of their gains annually by the tax code. As those gains are distributed, investors are taxed on them, and investors have seen this increasingly in the last few years as the markets have done well.

Portfolio design is an effective means of minimizing taxes. Investments may be taxable, tax-deferred, or tax-free. Investors should structure their portfolio so that they place the proper assets in each type of account. Generally, the same investments could go into any of those accounts—and so the question is whether they should.

This table illustrates the taxation of assets in each type of account.[18]

	Taxable Account	401 (k), 493(b), IRA account*	Roth IRA	College 529
Individual Stock	Taxed on dividends, capital gains if sold	All taxes deferred until withdrawal	Never taxed on growth or income	Not available
Mutual Fund	Taxed on dividends and capital gain distributions, capital gains if sold	All taxes deferred until withdrawal	Never taxed on growth or income	Never taxed on growth or income if funds used for college
Index Fund	Generally just taxed on dividends unless sold	All taxes deferred until withdrawal	Never taxed on growth or income	Never taxed on growth or income if funds used for college
Municipal Bond	Income is tax-free for federal, also for state if bond is from your state, taxed if you realize capital gains upon sale	Generally not held	Generally not held	Not available

18 * Notes: Tax penalties may apply on assets withdrawn before age 59½. See IRS publication 590 for a list of exceptions to the early withdrawal policy. Tax penalties may apply on earnings if proceeds are not used for qualified education expenses. See IRS publication 529 for a list of qualified education expenses.

Sometimes I meet prospective clients whose advisors have given them a portfolio that looks exactly the same in the taxable and tax-deferred accounts. This client's advisor was ignoring tax opportunities for the sake of simplification. Instead, you should have very tax-efficient assets (those that will not be taxed on an ongoing basis) in the taxable account. The tax-deferred account, in contrast, does not generate a Form 1099, and you have no immediate taxation on gains, so you would be less concerned about the tax status of the assets. There are exceptions to this, such as investors with tax loss carryforwards, but it all goes back to understanding an investor's situation.

For example, I would not usually put an actively traded stock portfolio in a taxable account, because you will be taxed every year on the gains as you buy and sell. More logically, it would go into a tax-deferred IRA or 401(k) and face no taxation on the trades. The tax savings can be significant. If you build a $1 million-dollar portfolio of investments in a taxable account and get 15 percent in gains distributed, that's $150,000 in capital gains. Your only choice might be to sell investments to cover the taxes, which might be $30,000 or more! In a tax-deferred account, no tax would be due until the funds are withdrawn.

In structuring a portfolio, you want to have assets in each of the tax status categories so that throughout your lifetime you can save, invest, and spend in the manner most advantageous to you.

Tax-deferred retirement accounts are a primary vehicle for tax-efficient savings. Almost everyone who has the opportunity should maximize their retirement accounts every year. It is a significant advantage to be able to reduce your taxable income that way. By deferring the taxes on your contributions, you have more money to invest. You are able to reduce your taxes during your working years while you accumulate money and are in a higher tax bracket. Then, in retirement, you are positioned to pay taxes at lower tax rates on the money you withdraw.

The future taxation of tax-deferred investments will of course depend on future rates and brackets. The presumption is that you will be in a lower bracket in retirement. In other words, you get deductions during a time when you are taxed at a higher tax rate, and you take your withdrawals during a time when you are taxed at a lower tax rate.

We have worked with a number of people in very high tax brackets who have been able to markedly reduce the current taxes they pay on their income by using two methods that go beyond the 401(k) plan:

- **Deferred compensation plans.** Corporate employees at the highest earning levels are often able to defer some or almost all of their compensation until after they retire. This is a great benefit. The tax rate on that income is likely to be much lower in retirement.

- **Pension plans.** Physicians and others who have small businesses can set up pension plans that allow them to set aside much greater amounts than are allowed in traditional retirement plans. Setting these up can be complex, but the potential benefits are enormous.

Tax-Free Capital Gains

If you are in the 15 percent bracket, capital gains are currently not taxed. That presents a valuable opportunity for early retirees to begin selling appreciated assets. Let's say you are in your sixties and are retiring, and you have assets in a taxable account that have appreciated over time. You can begin selling them free of tax on the gain, to the extent that your earnings do not rise out of the 15 percent bracket. Also, in the 15 percent bracket, qualified dividend income from individual stocks or indexes is also tax-free. Both are valuable strategies. Here is a table showing these attractive tax rates.

Ordinary Income and Dividend Tax Rate	Capital Gain and Qualified Dividend Tax Rate
10%	0%
15%	0%
25%	15%
28%	15%
33%	15%
35%	15%
39.6%	20%

Gifting Appreciated Assets to Children or to Charities

Selling appreciated positions is a logical part of rebalancing of a portfolio. Selling a stock and taking a profit is, of course, an important and rational part of the investment process.

What if you are selling a stock to make a charitable gift or to help a child with a down payment on a home? If this is the case, some other strategies can make sense. If you are charitably inclined, you will be much further ahead if you give appreciated securities to charities than if you sell them. Another option for people who would face high taxes on the sale of significantly appreciated securities is to gift them to their adult children. The children then can sell those securities and pay the taxes at their marginal rate—and, if they are in the 15 percent bracket, perhaps avoid the capital gains tax entirely. Likewise, you could shift such assets to your parents, and they could sell them with the same advantage if they are in a lower tax bracket. The transfer of significantly appreciated assets either to the previous or the later generation can certainly reduce taxation. If you are doing this, make sure you are doing it because you wish to gift, not simply to avoid taxes.[19]

Charitable Giving Strategies

Long ago, I opened a donor-advised fund, and I experienced the tax benefits firsthand. I quickly realized the potential for helping my clients, and I have since successfully set up donor-advised funds for many of them. Many of them donate $5,000 to $10,000 or more to charities each year, and this is a way to simplify their giving.

An easy way to think about a donor-advised fund is that it is basically a charitable account where the money is invested and grows tax-free. A donor contributes to the fund as frequently as they like and recommends grants to their favorite charity when they are ready to make the gift. A donor-advised fund is like setting up your own private foundation but without the complexity of having to file a separate tax return and provide all the documentation. And unlike

---

19 Note that the gift tax limit is $14,000 per individual or $28,000 for a couple in 2016. Gifts above this limit will use your unified credit. The unified credit enables you to give away $5 million (plus the annual inflation adjustments) during your lifetime without having to pay gift tax. By using the unified credit during your life, you'll reduce the amount available to offset the estate tax upon your death.

a foundation, you generally are not required to make a distribution every year and give away a certain amount of your assets.

It is a particularly useful tool for big earners. I may possibly advise a client to use this long-term charitable strategy to eliminate the payment of capital gains taxes for several years. In this hypothetical example, the client may have a $2 million taxable portfolio and decide to gift appreciated stock every year, donating an average of $75,000 annually through a donor-advised fund. This high level of philanthropy could have two great results:

- Avoid paying capital gains taxes and yet rebalance the portfolio by gifting appreciated positions. Capital gains realized in the 15 percent bracket are also federal tax free!
- Bring taxable income from $100,000-plus to the $50,000 range. When your taxable income is this low, you can do a Roth conversion using up the 15 percent bracket.

In this scenario, it would be a double win: supporting charitable causes and reducing taxes.

Donor-advised funds also make end-of-year tax planning simpler. Instead of making small gifts to different charities all year and keeping records of it all, you can simply transfer donations to the donor-advised fund and track them in one place. For example, if you go to a function and make a five-year pledge, you can set it up through your donor-advised account. The pledge will be managed by the company providing the donor-advised fund, and you won't need to worry about keeping track of it. Every year they will make the gift for you. IRS rules say a donor-advised fund cannot be used to fulfill a pledge, so this is more of a promise you are making to the charity than an actual pledge.

The donor-advised fund is also helpful if you don't know the cost basis for some of your securities due to lost purchase records.

You can gift the shares as long as you have held them over one year and cost basis is not needed.

In addition, you could prefund a donor-advised account during the accumulation phase of life and then make the grants when tax obligations drop during retirement. While waiting to direct the money to charity, you could do some more growth-oriented investing within the donor-advised fund.

You may set money aside for charity in a year when you have a high tax liability and want to receive the deduction and then actually do your gifting in some subsequent year. For example, suppose a number of my clients were departing employees of a large corporation and were paid significant sums in severance, potentially doubling their income for the year. The client may choose to open a donor-advised fund, contribute whatever amount they chose, and reduce their taxes through an itemized deduction by the amount of the gifts. In this example, some clients may have owned significant company stock with a low cost basis. They could gift the stock, receive the deduction for the donation, and also avoid the capital gains tax.

Despite those advantages of gifting appreciated securities, many people simply write checks to charities. Part of this is that many people actually do not have an investment portfolio. From a tax standpoint, gifting appreciated securities is much more favorable, and I encourage clients who have built up a significant amount of taxable assets to do so.

If, for example, you have a $10,000 gain on a $20,000 position, you likely will face a 20 percent or higher capital gains tax. By directly gifting rather than selling, you will have an additional $2,000 that you can use as you choose, perhaps also giving that money to charity through your donor-advised fund. The fund makes gifting those appreciated securities easier. Instead of the hassle of figuring out how to transfer shares to each charity, you gift the shares to the fund, and the donor-advised fund sends checks to the charities for you.

One thing that has happened for me with using a donor-advised fund is that it has helped me track who I am giving to and focus on giving more significant amounts to fewer charities. I think all of us realize we want to have an impact, and a lot of $100 gifts just do not help a charity like multiyear gifts of more significance.

Municipal Bonds[20]

Municipal bonds are another way for investors to minimize taxes. Basically, the interest on municipal bonds is tax-free. Yields are generally slightly lower on municipal bonds than taxable bonds, but the tax-free nature of the income is very helpful. Municipal bonds also have the virtue of having much lower credit risk (historically) than corporate bonds. The default rates on municipal bonds are very low, so the risk of losing your money has generally been low. Investors need to be cautious of investing in individual municipal bonds with high yields. For example, the city of Chicago, Illinois, is currently offering municipal bonds yielding 6 percent. When other bonds with similar maturities are yielding 3 to 4 percent, you must recognize that the bond has a higher degree of risk. In the city of Chicago's case, this higher risk is due to unfunded pension obligations.

Insurance Products and Annuities

Annuities are another way to get tax-deferred growth. You can buy an annuity with after-tax money, and it grows tax-deferred until you

---

20 There are risks associated with an investment in a municipal bond, including credit risk, interest rate risk, prepayment and extension risk, and geographic concentration risk. Income from municipal bonds is not subject to federal income taxation; however, it may be subject to state and local taxes and, for certain investors, to the alternative minimum income tax.

withdraw the money. Insurance products and annuities in most cases have slightly higher costs than other investments. The cost-benefit trade-off is worth considering. However, if you need liquidity, this might not be favorable for you, because you generally would pay a tax penalty on your gain if you take out the money before age fifty-nine and a half.

Annuities also generate ordinary income, so investors miss out on the tax-free options that are available on dividends and capital gains, as I mentioned earlier. Annuities have offered all kinds of guaranteed income options over the last decade.[21] In hindsight, some of the guarantees were attractive with the stock market challenges of 2000–2010. Generally, insurance companies have dramatically pulled back on the guarantees or raised the fees, recognizing that the offerings were not economically viable in turbulent markets. Investors need to understand the real rates of return on annuities. If you buy an immediate income annuity in your sixties, most of the income you receive is really just the return of your own money. To have these pay off and give you a reasonable return, you need to live well into your upper eighties.

Index Investing

In a taxable account, investing in indexes can be a particularly wise strategy. The S&P 500 is one of the most emulated indexes. The index consists of five hundred of the largest stocks in the US market. The index is not static—companies are acquired, go out of business, etc.—so the stocks in the index do change over time.[22]

---

21 Guarantees are based on the claims-paying ability of the issuing company. Surrender charges may apply for early withdrawal if made prior to 59½ and may be subject to a 10 percent federal tax penalty in addition to any gains being taxed as ordinary income.
22 Please note that although there are investments available that attempt to track an index, investors cannot invest directly in any index.

Charitable Strategies for IRAs

Charitably inclined investors should consider the tax implications when choosing the beneficiary of an IRA.

Let's say you have $1 million, half of which is in a tax-deferred account, such as the IRA, with the other half in a taxable account. By donating the tax-deferred assets, the charity gets the full $500,000. It owes no taxes because of its exemption. You could leave the taxable account of $500,000 to your children, and they would be able to sell the assets after you pass away without incurring capital gains tax. They could do so because the IRS allows them to "step up" the original cost basis of those assets to their current value, so they would not be taxed on the appreciation.

However, if you did it the other way and your children inherited the IRA, they would owe taxes on the lump-sum distribution, and the $500,000 bequest might leave them with only $400,000 after a 20 percent tax. The charity still would get $500,000 from your taxable portfolio, but the difference is this: In the first scenario, you transferred the full $1 million to family and charities, but in the second you transferred $900,000 to family and charity and $100,000 to the government.

You can see how the structuring of those beneficiary elections can make a significant difference. This might seem like common sense, but it doesn't always work out that way. People often leave the wrong assets to the wrong beneficiaries, with heirs paying a lot of unnecessary taxes. The tax code provides the opportunity for such savings, but it is up to you to take advantage of it.

Many attorneys draw up charitable bequests as part of a will or trust. For the very wealthy, this makes sense. We discourage this activity for many clients because IRA assets are ideal for charitable giving as we noted. Flexibility is another advantage of making your charitable gifts from your IRA. If the designation of funds changes over time (and we find it often does), you simply fill out a new beneficiary form. You do not need to visit an attorney and update your will or trust.

A very recent addition to the tax code allows investors who are over age seventy and a half to gift directly to a charity from an IRA. That gifting will satisfy the required minimum distribution that people must begin taking from their IRA when they reach that age. For those who are charitably inclined, this is a nice opportunity. What I am referring to here is gifting from the IRA during your lifetime, not as a beneficiary election. For individuals who either do not itemize deductions or do not get the full benefit of a deduction, gifting from the IRA makes a lot of sense.

IRA Stretch Provisions

Another possible strategy is leaving IRA assets to your children but not as a lump sum. Rather, you can take advantage of what is known as the *stretch provision*. This strategy allows heirs to extend the tax deferral beyond your lifetime. That way they can continue growing the account once it is theirs and receive income distributions from it.

If you are married, your primary IRA beneficiary is typically your spouse, who will directly inherit the asset. If your children are contingent beneficiaries and the IRA assets subsequently pass to them, they might choose to receive it as a lump sum. However, they would need to pay ordinary income tax on that distribution, and the sudden infusion of income could push them into a higher tax bracket.

Alternately, they could choose to receive the money as a *stretch* over their lifetimes. Ordinarily, IRAs cannot be tapped before age fifty-nine and a half without a 10 percent penalty, but in the case of inherited IRAs, that penalty is waived. Your child may have stopped working at age fifty and may have their own retirement plan in addition to the IRA that the child inherited from you. For income, your child could take distributions from the inherited account instead of his or her own and face no early withdrawal penalty. Be advised that inherited IRAs have minimum distribution requirements every year from the date they are inherited going forward.

Before leaving an IRA or any money to your children, you should consider whether they are capable of responsibly managing those assets. Of course, your children may be close to retirement age themselves, or perhaps they have already retired. You likely will have a good sense of how they will be able to handle the inherited money. You cannot mandate the stretch; they can choose to receive the money as a lump sum. If you are uncomfortable about the prospect that they might squander it, you could set up restrictions through a trust and have the trust distribute assets to your children over time. This does require the trust to be drawn up in a very specific way that will allow it to hold the IRA assets.

Roth IRA Strategies

In the 1980s, the government changed the rules on the deductibility of IRA contributions. If you already had a retirement plan and your income was high, you could no longer take a deduction for contributing to an IRA. As a result, IRA contributions slowed significantly.

To encourage retirement savings, the government created the Roth IRA in the late 1990s. It is different from the traditional IRA in that investors get no deduction for contributions, but their assets grow tax-free rather than tax-deferred.[23] It quickly became apparent

---

23 Tax penalties may apply on earnings withdrawn before age 59½. See IRS publication 590 for a list of exceptions to the early withdrawal penalty.

to me that my clients should put as much money as possible into a Roth every year. Tax-free growth is powerful, and the Roth is one of the best opportunities out there.

This works particularly well for investors who identify assets with huge appreciation potential and can put that money into a Roth. The value could increase tenfold, and they would pay no tax on that gain, as opposed to the significant amount that they would owe in a taxable or tax-deferred account. Most of us invest in a balanced portfolio in the Roth, but if you happen to identify a real opportunity, placing it in the Roth makes the gains tax-free!

In recent years, some employer retirement plans have included the option of a Roth 401(k) as well as the traditional 401(k) arrangement. For most employees who are given this opportunity, it makes sense to maximize the pretax contribution to the traditional part of the plan, thereby reducing the immediate tax liability.

Some retirement plans allow employees to set aside after-tax money in the 401(k). This is a significant benefit if you otherwise would not be eligible to open a Roth IRA. In 2015, if you are married and filing jointly with an income over $185,000 (this number changes slightly annually), you cannot contribute to a Roth IRA in a personal account. However, if the retirement plan with your employer allows an after-tax 401(k) contribution, you can take advantage of this and have some money growing tax-free. You just have to do a little two-step. Here are your choices:

- Keep after-tax dollars in 401(k)—assets grow tax-deferred
- Roll after-tax dollars out of 401(k) into Roth IRA—assets grow tax-free

A recent IRS provision allows you to roll after-tax funds out of a 401(k) every year directly into a Roth to capture this tax-free growth. It is up to you, however, to initiate that rollout, so you must actively manage your account. Otherwise, your earnings will simply continue to grow tax-deferred rather than tax-free.

If you do not have such a plan with your employer and your income level otherwise would disqualify you, there is another way to place money into a Roth. You may make a contribution to a traditional IRA without taking the tax deduction for it. Then you will be allowed to convert that money to a Roth. This conversion from an IRA to a Roth is another backdoor way to get funds into a Roth.

Here are the most common situations and the subsequent actions available to get money into a Roth IRA.

Income below Roth income thresholds	Contribute directly to Roth annually	This is the easiest and most common option!
Income above threshold, have no IRA	Contribute to IRA annually but do not take deduction	Convert IRA to Roth annually
Income above threshold, have a large IRA	Shift IRA assets into 401(k), then IRA has no assets, make annual contribution to IRA	Convert IRA to Roth annually

Let's say I had an investor who contributed to his IRA for many years in the 1990s. In this example, his income was too high, so he was not able to deduct the contributions to his IRA. He did not realize that all of the growth was becoming a tax-deferred asset while the contribution remained tax-free. (He could withdraw what he had contributed with no tax, but every dollar withdrawn would likely be treated as taxable in a ratio of the amount of contributions to the current balance.) His IRA had $60,000, of which about one half was his contributions and half was growth. When he was ready to retire, fifty cents of every dollar withdrawn was going to be tax-free, and the remainder would be taxable. In this example, I would convert the

IRA to a Roth IRA. This would result in the investor paying tax on $30,000 of gains now, but all future growth would be tax-free, not tax-deferred. This could also potentially put the investor in a position to do the backdoor Roth because he no longer has an IRA.

That probably doesn't make much difference if you're sixty-five years old. But if you are in your fifties and the money may not be withdrawn for fifteen to twenty years, you might have the funds double over this time, and all the growth would be tax-free. One of my goals is to help make clients' lives less complicated. This is a bit of a challenge since wealthy people have complicated lives! In retirement, trying to figure out which portions of your withdrawals are tax-free and which are taxable is an unnecessary complexity. That's just one more reason why it may be appropriate to convert assets with a mixed heritage of after-tax and pretax into a Roth, as a one-time transaction.

To accomplish more sophisticated strategies requires active engagement in your finances. You need to know what you are doing, or you need to work with someone who knows all the options. Some of these investment provisions are very recent, and you need to either personally stay on top of all the rule revisions or work with someone who does. If you do not understand the tax nature of your various assets and lack a plan for managing them, you almost inevitably are leaving money on the table.

Is a Roth always the best choice? You may not know until late in life. What you really need to think about is how you can diversify your portfolio by asset classes and how you can diversify the tax status of your portfolio. You have a lot of options to minimize your taxes when you have portions of money that are taxable, tax-deferred, and tax-free.

How Strategies Change as You Move from Working to Retirement

Once you retire or partially retire, your investment strategies may require revisions. Perhaps this year you are in a low bracket, and it would be more ideal to withdraw money from your IRA and pay the tax. In a later year, you may be in a higher tax bracket and receiving more pension and Social Security income. With these revisions, it might make more sense to take money from a taxable account and less from the IRA. Having your wealth in different buckets that may or may not be subject to tax on withdrawal gives you the flexibility to make decisions as things change. It is also very difficult to predict changes to the tax code in the future. The best approach is an agile one, so you are able to respond to meet your income needs with minimal taxes despite unpredictable events.

After you are seventy and a half years old, you will be required by the tax code to withdraw money from your IRA whether or not you need the income. If you're withdrawing IRA money and not spending it, then you really want to position it so that as it grows, you won't be taxed again. It is important to consider the strategies I mentioned so that your taxable account is more tax efficient.

The tax benefits that are written into the tax code were added to encourage favorable societal behaviors of investing, charitable giving, and home ownership. As a taxpayer, these benefits are available to you, but you are required to educate yourself or hire an advisor who can help you take advantage of them. The tax code has become much more complex in recent years. Unfortunately, many in the financial planning industry do not have a tax background and are not able to provide investors proactive recommendations. It is to your benefit to stay informed about changes to the tax implications of your investments. Working with a knowledgeable and competent advisor can save you that time and allow you to focus your energies elsewhere than on the tax code. At the end of this book you may be humored by my desire to see our tax code vastly simplified. I'm not trying to talk myself out of a job, nor do I believe I would be. I just believe our country is not well served by the tax code we have today.

CHAPTER 6

CREATING A LIFELONG INCOME

*Annual income twenty pounds, annual expenditure
nineteen pounds nineteen shillings and six pence, result
happiness. Annual income twenty pounds, annual
expenditure twenty pounds ought and six, result misery.*

CHARLES DICKENS

For eight years in the 1980s, I worked for Eastman Kodak, which at the time was one of the most recognized brands in the world. I left Kodak for a better opportunity, but I was wistful about leaving long-term friends and because I realized that I was saying good-bye to a lifetime pension and an era of retirement security.

In years past, people often would stay with the same employer for thirty or forty years and retire with a pension. Their retirement income was generally guaranteed through the pension plan, even if they had saved and invested very little on their own. Along with their Social Security benefit, this pension would provide a moderately comfortable retirement.

Today, many retirees who are in their eighties or older are enjoying a stable retirement thanks to a steady income from their pensions, their Social Security, and their own retirement assets. That was the traditional "three-legged stool" of retirement planning. For these retirees, their own assets have often only been used to cover desires such as travel, purchasing vehicles, and assisting grandchildren with college education expenses. Income from their pension and Social Security supports the majority of their day-to-day living expenses.

Good-Bye to Pensions

The pension leg began to fall off the three-legged stool of retirement planning in the 1980s, when corporations began freezing corporate pension plans and no longer allowed new employees access. Corporations recognized that they did not want to carry the investment risk of funding pensions. A good friend of mine in the auto industry shared with me that Ford and General Motors realized that the companies had become pension funds with an automobile division. Their pension funds were worth billions and billions of dollars—more than the actual market value of the automotive company. And it was actually more critical how they ran the pension fund than how they manufactured cars. This was not a desirable business model, with them having much less control of the investment results in the pension plan than in their automotive business. Like most corporations, Ford and GM have been trying to determine how to get out of the pension business. During the past decade, many companies have phased out pensions and, through 401(k) plans, have transferred the investment risk to their employees.

Today, few people under fifty years old have pensions. They may yearn for that sense of security, but it is not an option at most employers. This has created more mobility for employees, as they no longer feel tied to a company just so they will be vested in a pension. In planning for retirement, however, it has become incumbent upon them to develop their own retirement "pension" by creating an income stream from their own assets. Unfortunately, left to their own planning and without a pension's known income, investors often spend their retirement assets and end up in a tight spot in the latter years of their retirement.

The risk position of today's typical retiree is far different from that of pensioners, who generally have had a reliable income stream no matter what happens with their own investment assets and can afford to take more investment risk with corresponding higher potential gains. Those who must depend solely on their own investments as retirement income, however, may never recover from a significant drop in assets and could face a lifetime of lower income. That is what happened to many retirees in 2008–09.

How can retirees protect themselves from the possibility that they may run out of money? In general, they can invest in lower-risk assets. They can delay retirement, if possible, to build a bigger income cushion in the event of investment losses. Or they can build portfolios that generate significant income. This is more challenging today than in the past. With bond yields low, investors are forced to take on credit and interest rate risks to increase their income. We continue to focus on balancing sources of income to manage each of these risks.

Social Insecurity

The Social Security leg of the stool is clearly getting wobbly. For our clients in their early fifties, we project a 20 percent reduction in benefits, just in case the US government does not act to shore up the system. At one time there were over ten working adults for each retiree; today there are less than three.

The funds that are withdrawn from a worker's pay have historically been a transfer to the previous generation as retirement income. One way to understand this is that the Social Security that is deducted from your paychecks is effectively a transfer to your retired parents.

The Social Security system is funded as long as there are enough workers to support the number of retirees. As the number of workers declines and that of retirees' increases, the logical solutions to stabilize the program are to raise the Social Security tax, reduce the payments, or borrow money to pay the benefits. Currently, unfortunately, the government is choosing the borrowing approach. This obviously is not a sustainable way to fund benefits. All retirees, but particularly those in the future, will face declining or stagnant benefits to maintain the program.

I don't see the Social Security situation as disastrous. With changes in benefit levels and eligibility dates, the system can be stabilized. If elected officials in the US continue to delay authorizing small adjustments, more dramatic adjustments will be needed. Continuing growth of the US population is an important factor in the stability of the system. Should our population begin to decline, serious adjustments will be required sooner.

You might reasonably ask, "Whatever happened to the Social Security trust fund? I have been paying into it for thirty years, so where are those assets?" The unfortunate answer is that the funds you paid in over the last thirty years were immediately distributed to retirees. Social Security is still pay-as-you-go, with the difference being that future generations will pay for both the benefit outlay and the repayment of principal and interest on the special government bonds in the trust fund.

Meanwhile, runaway medical costs have made Medicare even more underfunded than Social Security. Medical costs at one time were not considered a major issue for many retirees. Much of corporate America once paid for retiree health care. This benefit is vanishing as the costs have risen significantly. Many individuals think that if they can just get to Social Security full retirement age, Medicare will take care of them and their costs will drop. Sadly, that is just not the case. A retired couple needs to plan to spend a minimum of $1,000 a month for medical expenses, and possibly much more, depending on their situation.

A common question among prospective retirees is when to begin taking their Social Security benefits. An entire book could be written on that topic. We suggest that when you are approaching age sixty-two, you should at least go to the Social Security office to review your options. Then we suggest visiting your financial planner to compare notes on what you have been told.

You have a lot of options, and properly handling the Social Security decision can result in a significantly higher lifetime income. We generally seek to have clients defer taking their payments until at least full retirement age, assuming they are in good health. The discounted payments you are subject to for taking Social Security at sixty-two are just too significant for most people.

When we began working with one couple, for example, we noted that the spouse's payments were about 25 percent of her husband's. We discovered that her payments were based on her own work history. She was not aware that she should be getting a spousal benefit amounting to half of her husband's benefit. She switched over to the spousal benefit, and for two decades now her income has been thousands of dollars more a year.

In recent years, many retirees have been using a strategy called "file and suspend" to maximize their benefits. As I write this, however, Congress has enacted dramatic changes that will make it more difficult for retirees to use these special techniques to maximize their Social Security benefits. The subject remains a moving target. Most financial planners know the rules and will advise you on your best choices.

Creating an Income Plan

More than ever, the third leg of the retirement stool—one's personal savings and investments—plays the central role in retirement planning. People are expected to be in charge of investing for their own future and creating the income they will need for the rest of their days.

That income will need to grow over time to cover the increasing cost of living. Eventually, retirees will find themselves spending less, which will cover part of the damage that inflation inflicts. As the years go on, people tend to travel less, buy fewer new clothes and furniture, and have fewer other discretionary expenses. Generally, retiree spending tends to be highest in the age range of sixty to seventy-five. It's not always the case—I have a client in his nineties who just completed an around-the-world cruise. That, however, is the exception to the rule. Discretionary spending tends to decline until the point when expensive long-term care may be needed.

The design of an income plan for retirement involves the interplay of assets with three primary characteristics: liquidity, safety, and growth. You need a certain amount of accessible, liquid money; you need to grow assets to cover inflation; and you need some degree of safety so that you will not worry about where you will get the money to pay monthly expenses.

A major consideration of income planning is to balance the sources for tax efficiency, as we discussed in the last chapter. Some people consider income planning to be as simple as turning sixty-two, switching on Social Security and perhaps a pension, and away we go. In reality, through proper planning you have a window between sixty and seventy where you can minimize taxes if you draw assets from the right pockets while possibly doing Roth conversions for tax savings even further down the road.

In your working years, you may have put a lot of thought into the value of deferring taxes until retirement. Now, in retirement, you still want to think about deferring taxes but also need to look at what tax bracket you will be in when you turn seventy and a half. Most of our clients will be in the 25 percent tax bracket at that point. As a result, we want to use up the 15 percent bracket in the early retirement years to move assets to Roth IRAs that we can later take out tax-free.

Interestingly, when needed, individuals who live conservatively are often more successful at reducing their spending than others. Spenders perceive many expenses as a need. They feel that they must spend and do not easily see opportunities to cut back. Spenders often have fixed obligations that savers avoid, like mortgage payments in retirement. Savers, in contrast, need to be encouraged to live a little and to spend their money. The mind-set is very different. We seldom run into retirement cash issues with savers. With spenders, it may be just a matter of time before they start to deplete cash. If you are a spender, you need to either accumulate a great deal of wealth or work on becoming more of a saver to avoid money issues in retirement.

Whether you are a saver or a spender, bonds serve two important primary functions in portfolios:

1. A counterweight to stocks that historically have gone up when the market goes down

2. An income generator to help provide retirement income

Ultimately, a strong income strategy requires investors to balance taking risks to generate more income with keeping bonds as a stabilizing factor in the portfolio. High-yield bonds, MLPs (master limited partnerships), and floating-rate bonds have all shown a tendency to act more like equities in periods of market stress. As a result, these higher-income investments are only appropriate for a smaller slice of an income portfolio.

The Total Return Approach

We use a total return approach to income investing that includes a combination of stocks, bonds, and other investments. You need to keep up with inflation, and so the portfolio needs to include growth assets as well as income assets. When we feel that the markets are more fully valued, our approach is to take some money out of the risk investments earlier than when it will be needed—perhaps six months to a year at the most. Using this method, we raise funds before they are needed and seek to avoid selling at lower prices.

Today it is just not possible for most retirees to construct a balanced portfolio of stocks and bonds that will give the 4–4.5 percent withdrawal rate most retirees need. The overall yield of a stock and bond portfolio is more likely in the 2–3 percent range. With both the S&P 500 Index and the ten-year US Treasury bond yielding less than 2 percent today, an investor needs to have a plan other than spending the yield to draw 4 percent. As a result, you need to plan to periodically sell assets that have given you growth to achieve that total return.

It is essential to track spending over time. Each year we track the percentage of the client's portfolio that is being withdrawn, and we monitor the trend. We want to see a withdrawal of 4 or 4.5 percent at most until clients are in their midseventies. If the client withdraws more than that, trouble is just a matter of time. Good markets can shelter retirees from excessive withdrawals for a while but not forever.

It is important to set up your income plan so that you take a fixed amount out of your portfolio monthly, similar to the fixed paycheck you earned at work. Retirees need to figure out how to live on that monthly amount and how to save some for the inevitable one-off expenses that we all have. For most people, surprisingly, we find that the one-off expenses are as much as 15 to 20 percent of the budget. So if a retiree tells us they can live on $10,000 a month, we probably need to budget $12,000 so cash builds up to pay the expenses they are not anticipating.

If clients come back to us every quarter needing more than we are sending to them, we look to see what can be done: Do we need to increase the monthly amount, or can they pare back their spending? Occasional spending overruns are not a problem during periods of strong market returns. However, during a market pullback, investors really need to cut spending. I have created a wealth worksheet to track assets, spending, and saving over time. The ability to see long-term trends makes it much easier to advise retirees on the sustainability of their spending.

In the wealth-tracking worksheet for Bill and Barb Smith, you will note the following:

- We track a client's tax situation every year; this gives us opportunities to do Roth conversions, take capital gains, do gifting, accelerate deductions, etc. In the example in the book, only three years are shown due to space constraints. We track all years.

- We note the sources of income, Social security, IRA withdrawals, income from portfolio, etc. to really understand the clients' income and income needs on a longer-term basis.

- We track withdrawals as a percent of assets. We are comfortable with an occasional spike to 5–7 percent but look to have withdrawals consistently be in the 4–4.5 percent range over time. Withdrawals above this are almost always trouble!

- We monitor overall wealth and how it is changing. Because of this we notice if for example a client was borrowing against their home to cover expenses!

Wealth Tracking Worksheet
Bill & Barb Smith

Bill	01/01/42	74					
Barb	01/01/41	75					

DESCRIPTION	12/31/13	Percent Change	12/31/14	Percent Change	12/31/15	Percent Change
Liquid Investments						
Cash and Cash Equivalents						
Cash and Cash Equivalents	$ 129,919		$ 124,564		$ 138,549	
Checking	$ 5,537		$ 7,601		$ 7,739	
Total Cash and Cash Equivalents	$ 135,456	-7%	$ 132,165	-2%	$ 146,288	11%
Investments						
Bill Smith Trust @ Raymond James	$ 431,367	27%	$ 466,764	8%	$ 426,998	-9%
Total Investments	$ 431,367	27%	$ 466,764	8%	$ 426,998	-9%
Total Liquid Investments	$ 566,823	17%	$ 598,929	6%	$ 573,286	-4%
Retirement Investments						
Bill's Retirement Accounts						
IRA @ Raymond James (Impac)	$1,356,123	32%	$1,333,248	-2%	$1,625,243	22%
IRA @ Raymond James (Ambassador)	$ 234,395	-37%	$ 260,438	11%	$ 274,358	5%
GIC	$ 311,965	-1%	$ 304,794	-2%	$ -	-100%
Subtotal	$1,902,483	11%	$1,898,480	0%	$1,899,601	0%
Barb's Retirement Accounts						
IRA	$ 13,259	23%	$ 17,369	31%	$ 17,801	2%
Subtotal	$ 13,259	23%	$ 17,369	31%	$ 17,801	2%
Total Retirement Investments	$1,915,742	11%	$1,915,849	0%	$1,917,402	0%
Total Investments	$2,482,565	12%	$2,514,778	1%	$2,490,688	-1%
Homes						
Residence	$ 625,000	-4%	$ 575,000	-7%	$ 575,000	-8%
Home Mortgage	$ -		$ -		$ -	
Net	$ 625,000	2%	$ 575,000	-8%	$ 575,000	0%
Total Homes	$ 625,000	-4%	$ 575,000	-7%	$ 575,000	-8%
Net Worth	$3,107,565	20%	$3,089,778	9%	$3,065,688	-1%
Change in net worth	$ 277,957		$ (17,787)		$ (24,090)	
	8.9%		-0.6%		-0.8%	
Raymond James Donor Advised Account	$21,000		$28,000		$24,000	

Tax Information

AGI	$122,000	$153,508	$139,342
Taxable Income	$86,685	$112,956	$99,512
Federal Tax Liability	$12,500	$17,341	$15,574
Federal Tax Bracket	25%	25%	25%
State Tax Bracket	1.5%		
Realized Gain/Loss	-$715	$21,361	$4,762
Gain/Loss Used This Year	$0		
Tax Loss Carryforward (at year end)	$0		

Income Sources

Social Security	$42,274	$43,138	$43,871
GIC Withdrawal	$12,835	$13,200	$13,310
Distribution from Trust Account	$12,000	$12,000	$12,000
Distribution from regular IRA Account	$60,000	$67,150	$69,725
Stock gifted	$11,916	$16,230	$14,544
	$139,025	$151,718	$153,450
Withdrawals from investments	$96,751	$108,580	$109,579
Withdrawals as a percent of assets	3.9%	4.3%	4.4%
Charitable Giving of stocks (Included in Withdraw	$11,916	$16,230	$14,544
	0.5%	0.6%	0.6%

The accompanying Wealth Tracking Worksheet was prepared solely to help you track progress on your personal financial plan. Accordingly, it may be incomplete or contain other departures from generally accepted accounting principles and should not be used to obtain credit or for any other purposes other than developing your financial plan. We have not audited, reviewed or compiled this statement.

This report is not a replacement for the official customer account statements from Raymond James or other custodians.

Investors are reminded to compare the findings in this report to their official customer account statements. In the event of a discrepancy, the custodian's valuation shall prevail. This data is furnished to you as a courtesy and for informational purposes only. This report may include assets that the firm does not hold on your behalf and which are not included on the firm's books and records. Although this data is derived from information which we believe to be accurate (including, in some cases information provided to us by you) we cannot guarantee its accuracy. This information is not intended and should not be used for any official tax, lending, legal, or other non-financial planning purposes and should not be relied upon by third parties. Performance data quoted represents past performance and does not guarantee future results. The investment return and principal of an investment will fluctuate so that an investor's shares when redeemed may be worth more or less than the original cost. The values represented in this report may not reflect the true original cost of the client's initial investment. Please contact your financial representative if there has been a change in your investment objectives, special restrictions, or financial circumstances.

Raymond James Financial Services, Inc.
Member FINRA/SIPC
Douglas B. Gross, CFP®, Financial Advisor
315 E. Eisenhower Blvd. Suite 301
Ann Arbor, MI 48108
Phone 734.944.7556

If you are a retiree facing the prospect of running out of money, you have a few options. You can reexamine your budget to spend less, of course. Or you can draw off some portion of your assets and put that money into a single-premium immediate annuity. If you are in your seventies, a single-premium annuity will typically pay a higher lifetime income than the 4 percent that we would suggest as a safe withdrawal rate. With part of your assets in the annuity and the remainder outside of it, you may safely be able to take a blended withdrawal rate more in the 5 to 6 percent range, which is above the 4 to 4.5 percent we like to see normally. The value of the annuity after you die, however, is zero, so typically you would put only a portion of your portfolio into a single-premium annuity. Basically, you have given that portion of your money to an insurance company in return for a better cash flow when you are alive, but you won't have that money to leave to your children or other heirs.

An advantage of a single-premium annuity is that you are taking away investment risk. The risk falls on the insurance company to make sure it has the money to pay you over your lifespan. That can make sense for people in good health who expect to live into their eighties or nineties. You shouldn't buy such an annuity if you are in poor health. You need to stand a reasonable chance of beating the odds.

Our current low-yield environment has changed much of the math of achieving an income in retirement. As a result, crafting an income plan and monitoring it may be one of the more critical times for investors to get advice.

CHAPTER 7

STRATEGIES FOR CORPORATE EXECUTIVES

Live so that when your children think of fairness
and integrity, they think of you.

H. JACKSON BROWN, JR.

We serve many high-level executives who lead busy and complicated lives. They receive an array of benefits that, if used properly, offer opportunities to minimize taxes, save more for retirement, and create significant wealth. Often, they accumulate a great deal of their wealth in a single stock—and along with the possible rewards come risks.

These employees need to make decisions on a variety of concerns, including how to manage incentive stock options and nonqualified options, deferred compensation, medical savings plans, 401(k) plans with before-tax and after-tax options, and employee stock savings plans.

To take advantage of all those benefits requires time and thought, but busy executives tend to focus first on work and family. We make sure they get solid information on their benefits. What are the key decisions to make on workplace benefits? Are they accumulating enough wealth and managing it properly? If they die, become disabled, or lose their job, are family members sufficiently protected? Those are just a few of the issues we seek to address in planning for them.

One of the major challenges faced by executives is understanding how their wealth accumulates. From one year to another it is not necessarily clear how much such an individual is saving, but over time the trends are clear. When you receive stock options, for example, exercising can make it look like your wealth is going down when you take the net value after the taxes you pay to exercise. Once people understand how significantly their wealth is growing, they can reach better decisions on saving and gifting.

If we were meeting with a corporate employee whose annual taxes were very high, in that $100,000-plus range, we would recommend looking at using a deferred compensation plan if it were available from their employer. It is key to look at the tax bracket you are in now versus the tax bracket anticipated in retirement. If you can defer taxes now while you are in the 39 percent bracket and withdraw them ten years later while in the 25 percent bracket you made a wise decision. We have seen individuals reduce their taxes very significantly through such deferrals.

Many factors should be considered before utilizing a deferred compensation plan. Individuals need to have the liquidity and cash flow first of all to defer the income. You don't want to defer the income and be tight for cash. It is also very important to consider the stability and credit rating of the company. You are essentially a creditor of the company. If they go broke, you may see just a fraction of the funds you have deferred at some unknown future date! We believe it is important to monitor your overall exposure to the company combining stock, stock options, RSUs, and deferred comp. An investor needs to be very conscious of this total exposure.

Once you get started deferring income, it is important to monitor the investments, keep beneficiary elections current, and make sure you are logically selecting the deferral period. This monitoring is essentially doing what you should already be doing with your other investments, with the additional complexity of the deferral period. Some of the deferral elections to monitor include: elections on death, severance, retirement, and change in control.

As you can see, there is a lot to examine, and that is just the deferred compensation portion. Generally, executives have a package of benefits that need to be considered individually and as a whole.

Asset Aggregation

An advantage of being an independent advisor is that we can choose the best tools to serve our clients. One of the software tools that we have identified to use is a productivity tool that updates client accounts more efficiently and revises their financial plans more judiciously. It is called eMoney Advisor.

Because executives often build wealth in a variety of places, they need a convenient way to track and update investments. With this software tool, investors are able to link and view their accounts for retirement plans, stock options, and accounts with multiple advisors. It provides the big picture; at any given moment, they can see exactly what they own. The aggregation program helps ensure that investors have reasonable weightings for each asset class over multiple 401(k)s, IRAs, brokerage accounts, and so on. It facilitates good investment decisions. We continue to evaluate tools that benefit our clients and improve internal productivity.

Managing Career and Stock Options and Restricted Stock Units (RSUs)

If you have stock options, you should have a strategy for exercising them and review it regularly. Investors need to understand the difference between incentive stock options, nonqualified stock options, and restricted stock units (RSUs) and have a strategy for each. Books are written on strategies for stock options; there is a lot of complexity here, and investors need to either really understand them or hire an advisor who does. Most companies have moved from awarding stock options to employees to restricted stock units in recent years for all but senior executives. Two of the factors driving the change toward RSUs are risk and complexity.

Risk

Stock options give employees the right to buy a company's stock at a specified "strike price" at a predetermined date in the future. When the stock market corrected in early 2000 and again in 2008, many employees found their stock options expiring below the strike price; the options no longer had any value and thus expired worthless. In 2008–09, the industry pared back on its parts suppliers, and many of those suppliers failed. That is just one example of why we emphasize the need for business owners to also own nonbusiness assets. Restricted shares, on the other hand, give an employee the full value of a company's stock at a future date. So even if the stock drops in value, they at least get that value when shares vest.

Complexity

RSUs are just a simpler form of compensation. When they vest, an employee can cash them out or hold the stock. The tax complexity of options leads many employees to hire a CPA simply to account for it.

Options do provide the greatest potential to generate wealth. Let's take a look at how options can work out, depending on your situation.

Suppose you are enjoying success in midcareer and have offers to join two firms. Company A is highly successful, with ever-increasing stock prices. Company B is struggling, and its stock has gone nowhere in ten years—but it wants to hire you to help turn it around. Each company would include stock options in your compensation.

You might think the stronger company would be the better choice, and perhaps it is. Think about those options, however: it is much better to be issued stock options at low exercise prices than at high ones.

Let's say you join Company A. Its stock is at a relatively high $50 when you join and remains flat for five years. You never exercise those options during that time, of course, because you would gain nothing.

Now suppose you instead join Company B and get options at $20 a share. The turnaround effort takes a few years, and you are issued options at $20, $15, and $10 over the first three years, with an average price of $15. If you received ten thousand options each time, you have a significant number of shares and would have some real money if the stock finally moved. If it got to $45, you would be looking at a gain of $30 for each share, or $900,000 before taxes. Compare that to the $0 you would have gained at Company A.

That's one reason why it might be worth considering employment with an out-of-favor company. There are many examples of high-ranking executives who made that decision. Alan Mulally left Boeing to join struggling Ford Motor Company. Mulally helped turn Ford around and was given millions of dollars of stock options at very low prices. Had he stayed at Boeing, his wealth would not have accumulated to that degree.

Of course, working at a struggling company to turn it around might also mean putting in sixty-hour weeks, traveling extensively, and missing time with your family. Anyone in such a position will evaluate the pros and cons and decide which path is best.

Recently, I was talking with a younger prospective client about his situation. He had done well, and in his forties he was starting to accumulate real wealth. He recently had left his firm and was looking to decide on the next opportunity. His children were ages six and nine, and he was fully aware of how fleeting those precious years can be. What's best for the family is certainly an important part of the decision. Rarely do you meet people who lament that they didn't spend enough time at the office.

The Prudent Path

Many people, as long as they are working and making an income, don't really do any financial planning. They're just going along. They do save, and they assume that they're saving enough. They basically live on their income and set money aside in a retirement plan, possibly up to the company match but rarely up to the maximum. Then sometime in their fifties, after they have sent their children to college, they ask themselves whether their current level of savings will generate enough income for them to retire. They come to us for answers. We, of course, wish we had talked to them in the decades prior, but here we are, and good decisions need to be made.

Often the answers depend on the desired retirement lifestyle. For individuals who spend what they make, it is difficult to accumulate enough assets to maintain the same lifestyle in retirement. Many times, the big spenders don't really have a budget. When there is money in the bank, they spend it. If the money isn't there, they borrow it. They always borrow for big-ticket costs such as home remodeling. Big spenders often find that they are forced to accept major changes in retirement because their assets will not support their accustomed lifestyle. To meet their goals, they would need to inherit significant funds or have some other financial windfall.

In contrast, retirees who have saved and live more modestly have a breadth of options. They may be able to buy a second home in a warmer climate, help out grandchildren with college, and take those dream vacations. They are in a completely different position.

For example, suppose a retired couple wants to buy a second home in another state to be near their grandchildren. After living modestly and saving for years, they still do not believe they are financially able to do so. Retirees who have successfully saved may also need advice on prudent spending. After reviewing their situation with their financial advisor, it becomes clear that they are able to purchase that home. What they needed was reassurance. With good counsel and good information, they may step comfortably into a retirement that may ultimately be a great source of joy for them.

CHAPTER 8

STRATEGIES FOR BUSINESS OWNERS

All our dreams can come true, if we have
the courage to pursue them.

WALT DISNEY

Business owners need to think about the day when they will hand over the keys to a new owner and settle into retirement. I have found that they often have not taken the time to plan sufficiently. It is critical that such planning start as early as possible.

When a business owner begins to contemplate retirement, the math is much different from that of the typical wage-earning retiree. Business owners first must work out a succession plan and a sales agreement. That could take years if they need to hire and train a successor who is capable of both buying and running the operation. The tax implications likely will be an issue in the sale, so business owners need to work with a good CPA and attorney.

Meanwhile, over the years, business owners need to reinvest in the company. That is the fastest way to grow wealth, but it also is the riskiest, as companies can fail. Some of that cash flow therefore needs to be invested in other areas, such as bonds, real estate, or stock investments. Real estate has been a significant part of the wealth of many of my business-owning clients. Owning the building that your business is in is a very logical and often profitable way to invest some of your wealth.

Creating those nonbusiness assets is essential. Small business owners often reach retirement age and find that the company just isn't going to sell for as much as they might have imagined. That is why they need to set aside assets elsewhere to provide for retirement. Many choose to set up tax-deferred retirement plans such as 401(k)s for themselves and their employees.

Business owners who have early success may ramp up their lifestyle and soon find that all the cash flow that comes from the business is committed to personal expenses. If they then experience one of the inevitable downturns that almost every business owner goes through, life can get complicated. A banking relationship and a line of credit can help the business to get by, but ultimately the best approach for business owners is to have excess cash and hang onto it. If you do this, a downturn can be unpleasant but will not threaten the very existence of your business. Money is like air to a business. We all have to breathe. Keep money in reserve, and life is much better.

Business Transition Strategies

People spend decades of their careers creating a business that produces tremendous wealth for them, but ultimately they need a plan to provide an income stream from that business in retirement. They will need to free up their nest egg to support them for the rest of their lives.

A few exceptional people do work well into their eighties and even their nineties. I have a client in Florida who simply did not want to transition out of his business and didn't sell it until he was over twenty years past normal retirement age. He liked what he was doing, and he felt that he owed it to his employees to keep the business going. His ultimate strategy, nonetheless, was to find a new owner with the capital to buy the business. There are not many like him. Most people expect to have been retired for a few decades at least by that age. To accomplish that, you need to put in place a business transition strategy.

One strategy is to arrange for an internal takeover of the business. If you have employees who are able to build up enough wealth to buy you out, that can be a wonderful solution for the continuity of the business and its management. Unfortunately, if you have succeeded in building a significant business, that is unlikely to happen. Your employees will not have the funds to buy you out. You will need to look for a third-party buyer, and you will need to prepare your business for the sale.

I have suggested to many of my business-owning clients that the best option for them may be to keep the business, hire staff who can largely run it, and incentivize them well. I know some business owners who have offered employees the opportunity to be paid a large part of any growth in profits of the company. This allows the owner to continue to be paid on the business's base income and for the employee to be well rewarded. Finding that person who can run and grow the business is, of course, your challenge. One of the reasons it may be advantageous to continue to run the business is valuation issues. A business owner may be offered as little as five to seven times net earnings for a business. If this is the case, you are a lot further ahead if you hire someone to run it and pay you the earnings.

Private equity can be one solution for the business owner who is trying to sell. Generally, private equity firms look to buy larger businesses, with sales of $10 million or more and profits of $2 to $3 million at a minimum. One of the challenges of working with private equity is that they generally want control. As a result, you may have just sold 51 percent of your business, and they are now in charge. If you are still working at the firm, the dynamics have now all changed. You are no longer in charge but are an employee. This may be quite an adjustment for entrepreneurs who have treasured their independence.

Most business owners do not have businesses of this size and will need to find a local buyer. One of the best options may be merging with a local competitor, and that's a good reason to cultivate congenial relationships.

A challenge for business owners is that they will generally have the potential to make more money in their business than they will in outside investments. That is because they control the decisions and the operations. We hope to produce returns of 5 to 10 percent a year for clients, depending on their risk tolerance and market opportunities. However, business owners could invest in their own company and leverage returns of 10, 20, or 30 percent in any given year. Obviously they could face losses, too. We saw that in our area among automotive-related businesses. In 2008–09, the industry pared back on its parts suppliers, and many of those suppliers failed. That is just one example of why we emphasize the need for business owners to also own nonbusiness assets.

In any case, business owners will need a strategy to transfer wealth into liquid assets to create spendable income for retirement. Diversification strategies include investing after-tax dollars in stocks, bonds, and real estate while also investing in a retirement plan within their business. We helped a medical practice establish a defined benefit plan that allowed them to set aside $300,000 a year for five years. Not only did that ramp up savings, but it also dramatically reduced income taxes through the tax deferral. That's the kind of creative solution that helps position business owners for successful retirement.

Estate taxes clearly are another major area of concern. Business owners should work with an experienced attorney to develop a plan that minimizes estate taxes. If you have been successful in business, ideally over time you have started to give shares to your children so that as the business grows significantly in value, it does so outside of your estate. Such advance planning makes a big difference in avoiding estate taxes. However, estate planning for business owners is rarely simple, and you should anticipate that family issues will arise. Let's say that most of the value of your estate is in your business, and only one of your three children is interested in and capable of taking it over. How do you treat all three children fairly in your estate planning? There is no perfect answer. It would be a poor strategy to give each a third of the business while only one runs it. There are strategies to help equitably distribute an estate, but they call for a lot of time and effort, and you would do well to seek the guidance of professionals in financial planning, taxes, estate planning, and other disciplines.

If you are grooming a successor, that will take time as well, whether it is someone within your family or a key employee. You cannot just decide to retire next year and expect the transition to proceed smoothly. You will need a team of professional advisors to help you pull it all together. Thinking about these issues in the early years of your business can be beneficial. Your plans likely will change over time, so you should revisit them regularly.

Having nurtured your business, perhaps for decades, you have made many strategic decisions to build it to what it is today. You understand your business intimately. It can be a challenge now to bring in someone who doesn't have the decades of experience and hope to get that person up to speed in just a few years. Even your children, as talented as they may be, will require a lot of work, patience, and time. It is important to clarify your expectations and goals, both short term and long term, and to implement any critical documents needed for the transition. You also will want to have contingency and insurance plans in place in case anything should happen to you.

How will you know how much your business is worth? Depending on the type of business, there are many ways to come up with its value. CPA firms generally do a good job of valuation. It is important to be working with a CPA all along to structure your business properly. For example, will it be an LLC or a corporation? The tax implications are significant.

The structure of the sale itself also will depend on a variety of factors, such as whether it is within the family, with a key employee, or with an outside buyer. Your children may be the right people to take over the business, but don't presume that they will survive you. And what if they get divorced? You can anticipate such possibilities and structure the sale to protect your children, the business, and yourself. Ultimately you will need to receive enough from the deal to support you in your retirement, particularly if you have not created other nonbusiness assets. Will you be paid in a lump sum? Will you be paid over time?

The nature of the business may determine the answer to some of those questions. If you are running a business where your skills and personality are intrinsic to the value, it may be challenging to pass it on to a successor. Your customers may see you as the institution and the brand, and they may not want to patronize the establishment once you are gone. If you have agreed to receive money over time, you may find yourself in a position where your successor can no longer make the payments. In this case, the business is back in your hands—and you're seventy years old. For that reason, you may not wish to play the role of creditor to a purchaser. And you certainly want to have nonbusiness assets for your retirement.

As you can see, the process of retiring can be particularly complicated for business owners. Careful planning is important for anyone, but you face additional issues when you run a business. The earlier you start saving and creating outside assets, the better. This can dramatically reduce your reliance on a "home run" sale of the business. I have had clients who sold for big money and it all worked out, but I have also seen businesses go bankrupt at about the time the owner was hoping to retire. Business owners have a lot of options, but much can go amiss. Careful planning will greatly enhance the chances of fulfilling your retirement dreams.

CHAPTER 9

INSURING YOUR FUTURE

Taking care of what's important.

My grandparents died in a car accident when my father was only eight years old. Such tragedies can devastate families for years, and yet my father and his brother had the resources to make it all the way through college. My grandfather, a patent attorney, had the foresight to protect his family with sufficient life insurance.

I have often met people in their thirties and forties who are making good money in a promising career—yet they have not taken into account the possibility of something happening to them. They feel that they are providing well for their families, and they do indeed keep the paychecks coming in. But how would their families fare if those paychecks ceased for some reason? It has happened countless times: the phone rings in the night, and everything is changed.

Life Insurance

In my career, I have known widows who were in their forties when their husbands died. They had a reasonable amount of life insurance, but they could have had more, or they had been sold a small permanent insurance plan.

An agent gets a much higher commission by selling permanent insurance, types of which include whole life, universal life, and variable life. These certainly are viable types of insurance, but people often purchase permanent insurance when what they really need is a term policy.

Permanent insurance often is sold to young people as a means of building wealth—as an investment as well as income protection. In my career as an advisor, I have never had a client come in with an insurance policy that has worked out meaningfully as an investment. Some have built $20,000 to $100,000 of cash surrender value over decades, but they have also not had the amount of insurance they needed to protect their families. Let's say I have an executive in his fifties come in; he has been paying $1,000 per year for a whole life policy, and his death benefit may be only $25,000! If instead he had purchased a term policy, the same outlay might have given him $500,000 or more of coverage! The only cases where I have seen a permanent policy generate real wealth are when a mutual insurance company converts from ownership by policyholders to ownership by shareholders. The policyholders then receive stock, which can be a significant windfall. However, I would not buy insurance and wait for that to happen.

A term policy, which provides a much higher level of benefits, protects your family for a specific period while you are building your savings. Term insurance is less expensive for two main reasons—in almost all cases the policy term ends long before the insured dies, and it does not build a cash value. It is very inexpensive for nonsmokers who are in good health. Term insurance is a particularly wise strategy for young families in which one spouse does not work or earns significantly less than the other.

We recommend that our clients obtain term insurance until they build up enough assets to drop it. The term lasts as long as the risk; a lot of clients recognize that when they reach their late fifties and early sixties, they no longer need this coverage. Here is a chart illustrating this relationship: as your wealth grows, your insurance need declines.

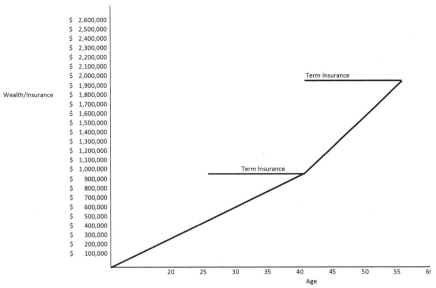

In this example, a twenty-five-year-old buys $1,000,000 of insurance when they begin to have children. Over time, their wealth grows to $1,000,000, but their income and insurance needs have also grown. Now, perhaps at forty, they buy a new policy of $1,000,000 of insurance that they carry until in their late fifties their wealth has grown to $2,000,000. At this point they no longer have an insurance need.

Successful people often do not realize how underinsured they are. They think they are in good shape if they have a policy that provides coverage for three times their earnings or at most five times. It's far from enough. This is a particularly acute problem among highly successful business people. The reason they are underinsured is that they started out making $50,000 or $100,000 a year and now find themselves making $300,000 to $500,000 a year, but they have not revisited the insurance issue. In this case, their assets are typically far behind their income because their salary recently jumped.

It can be difficult to grasp how much money it will take to replace your income if you were to pass away. I have often met people in their forties who are doing well, but if they died, their spouse's lifestyle would suffer. It is important to get a professional evaluation and not simplistic guidance like "The amount of your life insurance should be seven times your income." Think carefully about your assets, liabilities, special needs, and how long you will need protection. This analysis is how you determine how much coverage you should purchase.

We help clients project the time required to accumulate adequate assets so insurance will no longer be necessary. For example, if you reach the point where you are sixty years old with $4 million in assets and know that you are on track for your desired retirement income, then you may not need to continue to purchase life insurance. However, when you are forty years old, make $400,000, and are building your wealth yet have only acquired a half million dollars in assets, you will need life insurance, likely at least $3 to $4 million worth, to make up the gap. As your wealth builds, you can gradually cut back the amount of life insurance.

It is important to take good care of your health—not just so that you will live longer, which is of course the prime benefit, but also because you will save a lot of money on your life insurance. If you smoke, for example, the cost of your insurance will be two to three times higher than for a nonsmoker. For $1,000 a year, a client in their forties in great health could buy $1.5 million in life insurance, perhaps even $2 million. A smoker would spend at least $3,000 for that same policy. So the cost of a pack of cigarettes is actually far more than the amount that the smoker spends, not to mention the opportunity cost of years lost from a life cut short.

Permanent insurance does have a purpose, so please do not take my criticism of it as meaning that it never makes sense. Permanent insurance is named as such because it is insurance that you have your entire life. It is primarily used today as an estate-planning tool and is very effective as such. As I mentioned earlier, I do not see this as an investment vehicle. The cost of insurance simply makes it a less effective way to invest. I have some more notes on permanent insurance in Chapter 11, on "What You Leave Behind."

Life insurance policies have exclusions and/or limitations. The costs and availability of life insurance depend on factors such as age, health, and the type and amount of insurance purchased. As with most financial decisions, there are expenses associated with the purchase of life insurance. Policies commonly have mortality and expense charges. In addition, if a policy is surrendered prematurely, there may be surrender charges and income tax implications. Guarantees are based on the claims-paying ability of the insurance company.

Long-Term Care Insurance

Long-term care insurance is appropriate for many people, but if you have accumulated adequate assets to support your lifestyle, you should consider self-insuring. If you are living on a retirement income of $150,000 to $250,000 a year, you are in a position where you can afford the cost of long-term care out-of-pocket, should it become necessary. Your expenses inside a nursing home probably would be less than your expenses outside. People worry about that situation where they get Alzheimer's and are in a long-term care situation for many years. We discuss family histories with clients, and if Alzheimer's is a risk, we discuss the cost and trade-offs of insurance versus self-insuring.

Certainly, there are people who spend a long time in a nursing home, but they are the exception, not the rule. The premise that you must have long-term care insurance does not necessarily make sense for wealthy clients.

Frankly, a good relationship with your spouse and maintaining a great marriage is one of the best forms of long-term care insurance. The reality is that there are many couples where one of the spouses would be in a nursing home, except that the other is able to provide loving care. That works when the spouse who needs help is still relatively mobile and when the caregiver still has sufficient energy and is up to the challenge, perhaps with some outside help. Spouses who are dedicated to looking out for and taking care of each other can live independently for much longer.

Most of my clients who are wealthy are used to very independent living. They don't anticipate that they will be going into a nursing home and will do what they can to stay out. Those who have needed assistance have been able to hire people to come to their homes. They are able to remain independent, in some cases until hospice care is needed. For many clients, long-term care coverage gives them a sense of security knowing that there will be funds available to take care of them. As advisors, we certainly think it is important to review clients' feelings about long-term care and to offer a cost-effective policy if they are interested.

Guarantees are based on the claims-paying ability of the issuing company. Long-term care insurance or asset-based long-term care insurance products may not be suitable for all investors. Surrender charges may apply for early withdrawals and, if made prior to age fifty-nine and a half, may be subject to a 10 percent federal tax penalty in addition to any gains being taxed as ordinary income. Please consult with a licensed financial professional when considering your insurance options.

Umbrella Coverage

You obviously will need auto and home insurance, but you should also consider what is known as an *umbrella policy*. As people build wealth, their prosperity means that they face a greater potential that they could be sued. An umbrella policy covers you in the event that a lawsuit seeks damages that exceed the limits of your auto or home policy. This is no small matter. A lifetime of savings could be at stake. A $1,000,000 umbrella policy can cost as little as $200 a year. This is a lot of protection for your wealth.

CHAPTER 10

....

INVESTING WISELY

I will tell you the secret to getting rich on Wall Street.
You try to be greedy when others are fearful. And
you try to be fearful when others are greedy.

WARREN BUFFETT

As I was writing this book, I found myself typing a long chapter about lessons for investing, including all the mistakes and successes I have seen over the years. But then I stepped back, realizing that you, my readers, would not be looking for a tome on investing. You would not be reading this book if you were planning to manage your own assets. This is not to say that many of my clients are not capable of managing their assets—generally they simply choose to spend their time on their careers, families, and other interests.

Investing can be interesting, challenging, and humbling. The investment "lessons" that you learn in one decade may be entirely wrong in the next. In the 1990s, every dip was a buying opportunity. Buying on dips in the following decade worked, but it took a lot more patience, and the drops were much more painful and long-lasting. The current lesson that the markets seem to be teaching is that investors should just index their money because active management generally hasn't been beating the markets.

Investors need to be cautious about assuming that's the correct approach for all their money.

Our approach to investing consists of building diversified portfolio models and using a combination of active and passive mutual funds and ETFs (exchange-traded funds). We have had solid long-term success in keeping clients invested at a risk level they are comfortable with and that over time should allow them to reach their goals. Successful investing is measured over decades. Investors who become frustrated if they don't "beat the market" every year will find themselves changing advisors and strategies every few years, seeking that perfect solution.

We also invest in individual stocks, something many advisors are moving away from. Our feeling is that it is important to have a real understanding of markets, and owning individual stocks gives this understanding. If all you own is funds, you may really not understand why your fund is outperforming or underperforming—it is all about the individual stock holdings in the fund. Owning individual stocks also helps us when we go to advise clients with large individual stock holdings on their strategy.

Real Estate Investing

Buying real estate at low prices is one way to potentially earn outsized returns. The multifamily building that Sabrina and I purchased in Tecumseh, Michigan, in 1989 worked out well for us because we bought it when prices were low and the economy was flat. We paid $110,000 for it, put $50,000 into the remodeling over the next five years while collecting rent that paid the mortgage, and then sold it for $210,000. Clearly this was in a small town and a long time ago!

It was a profitable investment, but it also took a lot of our personal time. Sabrina contends we did not make money on it, but I think that is because she is counting the value of all those hours spent!

After this experience, I realized that I would prefer to buy a stock that may have the potential to double in five to ten years rather than invest in real estate, which takes more time to manage and has less liquidity. Real estate does have powerful advantages as an investment, as it provides both leverage and tax minimization. But for me, the time required overwhelms those advantages.

Control through personal management of the investment is another clear advantage of privately held real estate over individual stocks. As an investor, you need to think about the opportunity that is in front of you and how you want to spend your time. Are you entrepreneurial? Do you live in an area where there are great real estate opportunities?

Most areas have real estate opportunities at different times and in different types of properties. You first need to determine if you have the time and skills to identify the type of properties that would be advantageous and to then manage the properties. Just be mindful of the value of your time, and of course, be aware of the risks.[24] An investor thinking about real estate should be reading extensively to thoroughly understand this type of investing.

Condos versus Homes

Investors need to remember that location and uniqueness are among the most valuable features of real estate. Condos may have a great location but are rarely unique; there are multiple units in the same

---

24 Real estate investments can be subject to different and greater risks than more diversified investments. Declines in the value of real estate, economic conditions, property taxes, tax laws, and interest rates all present potential risks to real estate investments.

building and often new and more attractive buildings being constructed, even in areas with limited real estate. As a result, appreciation of condo real estate is rarely as good as that of single-family homes. Clearly, in some areas you cannot afford or even find a suitable single-family home, so this is not really an issue. I will share a friend's experience as an example. I shared a condo with a friend in Perrysburg, south of Toledo, Ohio, in the late 1970s. He sold the condo for about $50,000 when he moved away. He moved back to Perrysburg ten years later, after a period of relatively high inflation. His condo was for sale again for nearly the same price as a decade earlier. If a condo is your best option, be sure to look into the annual fees and association management. An underfunded condo association reserve can lead to lots of unexpected future expenses.

Opportunities Disguised as Investments

Most of us understand the difference between an asset and a liability. Assets make money; liabilities cost money. To build wealth you want to invest in things that grow in value rather than assets that have high expenses and probably will have modest appreciation. Remember, the point of an investment is to make money. It should not be something that might allow you to break even but will probably cost you money. Let's take a look at some things that are sold as investments but are not.

A SECOND HOME

Investors often wonder whether they should buy a condo in Florida or at a ski lodge or perhaps a cottage at the lake. A second home or a vacation home is an attractive idea if you want a place of your own to stay when you travel to your favorite places. You may forecast that you will rent the property for the remainder of the year—but the challenge is that, typically, rental demand is seasonal, and units often will sit empty for six months or more out of the year. You need to charge premium rents during the high season, and this means that you are not able to use it during this time.

If you have the resources to afford a vacation property, that's wonderful, as long as you understand that this "investment" could well be a financially unproductive one. It can be expensive to maintain as well. A lake cabin, for example, requires a lot of work to prepare it for a high season, which may only last a few months. If there is any risk of freezing water lines, you will need to winterize it.

I own a small summer cottage in Michigan that my family and I enjoy, but I am not under any illusions that it is an investment. The reason to buy a vacation property should be that you and your family will be using it often for your own pleasure. Be cautious about convincing yourself and your spouse that a seasonal property is an investment. The family time at the cottage for all of us is priceless, but it is not inexpensive. Certainly on occasion investors buy such properties during deep recessions, and they can be investments. Timing is in this case critical, and you may need to sell it when it appreciates to minimize the costs that will drag down your returns over time.

From 2005–07, beachfront condominium developers in Florida sold top-floor units at what they promoted as attractive prices to those who committed to buying them before the buildings were completed. While the real estate market was still hot, some buyers quickly resold their units at a nice profit.[25] Some speculators waited too long, and they felt the pain of a million-dollar condo selling for $500,000. When an investment appears too good to be true, it

---

25 Abby Goodnough, "As Condos Rise in South Florida, Nervous Investors Flee", New York Times, May 26, 2007, http://www.nytimes.com/2007/05/26/us/26condo. html?_r=0.

probably is. For the person who bought at the bottom in 2008, the condo may work out as an investment if they sell in a few years. Held long term, the costs of condos tend to overwhelm the appreciation.

TIMESHARES

When buying a timeshare, you are buying access to a resort and, in theory, fractional ownership of a property. It's nice to have the prospect of locking in a desirable week every year at accommodations that are much better than a hotel room. However, consider the downsides:

- Timeshares have high annual maintenance fees.
- It may take a lot of effort to actually snare a desirable week, as high season weeks are in strong demand.
- Your ability to resell the timeshare is, in many instances, nonexistent.

You're better off if you do not think of timeshares as an investment. Think of it as prepaying some of your vacation costs with the chance to lock in a desirable location and week. Be sure that you understand the long-term costs. Consider whether you might be better off using the money that you spend on a timeshare to invest elsewhere. However, sometimes you simply cannot get a hotel that in any way compares to what a timeshare offers at a particular location. In that case, a timeshare is certainly less expensive than purchasing a condominium.

PERMANENT LIFE INSURANCE

I must highlight here a point that I made in the last chapter: the purpose of buying insurance is to protect you and your family against some risk. That might include the risk of dying too soon or being held liable for damage to property or claims in a lawsuit or of estate taxes diminishing an estate. Most of those risks may be best addressed with various types of insurance policies, such as auto, home, and term life insurance. Permanent life insurance is an effective investment to protect your estate, but I do not believe it is an effective investment to save for college, retirement, or some other future income need. Term insurance and permanent insurance each should be used for its own best purpose.

CARS

Cars are not investments. They are tools allowing you to get to work, run errands, and take trips. Cars have operating expenses and depreciate in value and therefore are an expense that most of us must incur.

My advice is to always buy good used cars that you can get at a discount and then drive them for a long time. Many people get lured into buying an expensive new car, going $50,000 or $60,000 into debt. Unless you are quite wealthy, it makes no sense to spend such money on a depreciating asset, particularly one that plunges in value the moment you drive it off the lot. If that money were set aside to grow, it could multiply several times over the years and contribute to a prosperous retirement.

I confess that I bought a new car when I graduated from college. So did my wife. New graduates often feel they deserve such a treat, but I was less enthusiastic about my purchase as I watched it depreciate 50 percent in value within a few years. For many years I have purchased cars that were a few years old, at a nice discount from their original price. I certainly am not opposed to enjoying attractive belongings, but I want to get them at a reduced cost, and I am cautious about devoting resources to anything that I know will lose its value. I still occasionally buy a new car; to make the economics work, you need to hold it for a long time and maintain it well.

CHAPTER 11

WHAT YOU LEAVE BEHIND

Death is not the end. There remains the litigation over the estate.

AMBROSE BIERCE

Y|ou likely have heard about estate-planning fiascoes among celebrities, where money was squandered in taxes and other expenses as family members squabbled. Often, much of the heartache could have been prevented by thorough and thoughtful advance planning.

How will your estate be managed if you become incapacitated or die? It's critical to identify a trusted person capable of managing your estate. That person often changes over time. When clients are in their fifties, they might designate a sibling. By the time they are in their eighties, that sibling may be deceased, so they designate one of their children or some third party, such as a trust company, to handle the estate.

Those decisions are a matter of confidence and capability. Do your children have the ability and time to settle your estate? Some people are terrific at this, and we have seen it work out just fine; other times it's a burden to them. You may be better off using a third party. You have to pay a cost for that service that may run 2 percent of the estate or more, but that can be insignificant when you consider that it relieves your children from dealing with all those matters after your death.

Like a financial plan, an estate plan is typically customized and then modified over time. For a young, newly married couple with few assets, estate planning may consist of just beneficiary designations on retirement assets and life insurance. As time goes on, the addition of children and growth of assets require more serious estate planning. You want to have a plan for who will take care of your children if you die and a plan for the disposition of your assets. Estate plans require a lot of thinking through of possible scenarios and planning for each one. Much of the most complex planning is done during these years, when children are younger, we are not sure if they will responsibly handle assets they might inherit, and you may be concerned about who they will marry.

When people get up into their eighties, the estate plan may become less complex. For example, imagine a married couple who feels comfortable planning to divide their assets among their responsible, adult children. The couple may set up a transfer, upon death, of their personal accounts and beneficiary designations for 401(k)s and IRAs or other retirement accounts. In this simplified case, they may just have a will, which provides for the disposition of their home and miscellaneous minor assets. For people in this type of uncomplicated situation, the preparation of their estate plan requires less analysis. Our practice has been seeing more elderly clients who elect to take that route.

In simpler estates, an attorney can set up several key documents that most people should have. Those include your will; a trust, if necessary and desired; powers of attorney to handle your financial and medical affairs if you should become incapacitated; and a living will to direct the extent to which you want medical intervention if you are near the end of life.

The use of a trust becomes more important when people have more complicated assets and situations. Perhaps their children are still young and have not yet demonstrated their ability to handle money. Or perhaps they have demonstrated shortcomings in handling money. Either way, Mom and Dad may want the money distributed over time, with restrictions. They also may want to protect the value of the estate from a divorce claim, particularly if a child has recently married and the stability of that union seems problematic.

In such cases, the estate plan may be designed to distribute assets to the children gradually, with a custodian sending them checks based on the established provisions. The children could get money upon graduation from college, for example, or attaining some other milestone. The goal is to ensure that the money will be used wisely and not squandered. We all have heard stories about lottery winners who quit their jobs, go on a spending spree, and within a few years, their lives are a wreck and they are broke. Some people will likewise misuse a large and unbridled inheritance.

This is a particular concern for people who have built significant wealth. Most people do not have an estate so significant that they will be worrying about whether the inheritance will spoil the children. Nonetheless, those who will be passing on a sizable estate will do well to consult with an attorney, a CPA, and a financial advisor to go over the options.

You also need to make sure that all pertinent accounts are properly titled in the name of the trust in order for it to work most effectively. People have been known to draw up estate plans but continue to have their personal taxable accounts in joint name. When they do this, the assets must still go through probate.

Having a trust was once the chief means by which people avoided probate. Now, it has become much easier to avoid probate simply by designating "transfer on death" for accounts that are not set up with beneficiaries, such as taxable accounts. Avoiding probate is not as big an issue as it once was, but many people remain concerned about privacy. Probate proceedings become public knowledge. If you wish to avoid probate and keep your estate settlement private, you will want to set up a trust and have your assets titled in the name of the trust.

Another common reason for having a trust is to seek better control of what happens to your assets when you are in a second marriage and you die. You will want to make sure that your assets go where you expected. This can be a particularly difficult issue when each party has children from a previous union. An estate plan can be all drawn up, but after the death of the first spouse, the survivor may decide to have the marital assets to go to his or her own children. In one possible scenario, the owner of an IRA may have designated the money to go to his son. The spouse, however, has power of attorney on the IRA. If the owner is incapacitated, she has the ability to move the IRA to another provider and establish a new beneficiary—namely, herself and her children (which did not include the designated son of the incapacitated husband).

Just be aware that if you become incapacitated and your spouse has intents that differ from yours, a situation such as that could arise. You might think that your spouse would honor your wishes, but people do surprising things. The way to protect your intentions is to establish a trust with a third-party trustee to manage things such as that IRA if you become incapacitated. You can arrange distributions to your spouse during his or her lifetime, but you can also make sure that your intended beneficiaries will get the assets.

Again, the degree of complication depends upon your situation. The bottom line is that you will want your assets to go where you have designated in the manner that you set forth. That is not necessarily a simple accomplishment, but with careful planning you can rest assured that your intentions will not be undone. If you are using your trust as a beneficiary of your IRA, you need to be sure that it is properly designed to maintain the assets, tax-deferred, after you die. If the trust is not designed as such, all the assets will come out of the IRA at death, and a large tax bill will be due at that time. A properly designed trust, often called a *see-through trust*, prevents the tax debt and allows the assets to continue on, tax-deferred, being distributed to your heirs over time.

Dealing with the Estate Tax

The estate tax can be onerous for high-net-worth families. For 2016, the federal exemption was $5.45 million for an individual, meaning that estates would face a 40 percent tax on values exceeding that amount. For married couples, the exemption is twice that figure, so most estates do not have to pay the federal tax. Highly affluent families will be subject to the 40 percent tax and need to carefully plan to reduce that tax as much as possible.

There are many strategies the wealthy use to minimize estate taxes. One of the simpler strategies is to purchase permanent life insurance and have that become an asset outside of the estate. That is one of the preferred methods for many people; they buy life insurance in sufficient quantity to pay the estate tax when it is due upon their death.

For people of tremendous wealth, the strategies can become quite involved, and they need to identify and take advantage of numerous opportunities to reduce their taxes. It is not the purpose of this book to explain all of those strategies and maneuvers. That is a matter for them to take up with attorneys who specialize in estate planning.

Reviewing Beneficiaries

People who neglect to take care of the estate-planning basics take the risk of unfortunate experiences. Many people do not realize that a will does not control what happens to assets with beneficiary designations. If you have an IRA, the investment firm will not ask for a copy of the will to decide who gets the money. They have instructions through your beneficiary designations and will send them the money when you die. An example of this would be a situation where a client contacts me after her husband has died. If some past girlfriend or other acquaintance is named as beneficiary of the husband's IRA they will get the money, regardless of how long you have been married or what the will says. The girlfriend has the option of keeping the money as IRA beneficiary although the deceased may have had different intentions.

It is essential to keep track of the beneficiary designations on a retirement plan. In working with our clients, we make sure that those are examined and updated if necessary. Those designations take precedence over any wording in a will or trust. Once the owner of the plan is deceased, there is no way to change the beneficiary. The mutual fund or investment company must honor it. (I'm repeating myself for emphasis!)

In other cases, it is important to review those designations because they are unnecessarily complicated. The estate tax exemption once was much lower than it is today. In 2000, for example, it was about $650,000, so people set up complex designations to keep money out of their estate. Because the exemption today is far higher, it is important to review those designations to make sure they are still logical. With the higher exemption, you now may want the money to go directly to your children for example where you previously had some complex plan.

You may also want to use your IRA beneficiary election as a convenient and uncomplicated means for leaving a bequest to charity. Charitable intentions often change over time. People develop new interests, or they move to new communities. Let's say that at age sixty you have been actively involved in a particular charity, and so you decide to leave money to it in your will. That bequest will come from the taxable assets in your estate. But when you are seventy, that charity matters less to you. You have moved on in life and decided to support different causes. To change your gift, you need to go back to an attorney and get your will rewritten. Alternatively, you can use your IRA beneficiary election to make your charitable choices. If you change your mind, you just file a form, and you're done. It costs nothing, and it is far simpler than changing your will and trust.

More than the Money

As people who have attained wealth get older, they often will want to bring in the family for a consultation. For some of our wealthier families, we conduct an annual planning meeting with the family to talk about the estate, review it with the attorney and the CPA, and make sure that everyone understands the purpose and goals, the overall business situation, and what will happen if and when family members pass away.

By getting together that way, you encourage family unity and can make sure that everyone, including the professionals, is on the same page. That will markedly improve the chances that your financial desires will be honored.

It is not all about the money, although no doubt that will be the topic for much discussion. You are passing on your values, your ethics, and the stories and memories that have made your family unique. That is an important part of your bequest to your children and grandchildren. When they know and cherish the role that their elders played in creating the wealth, they are far more likely to treat it with respect—and that certainly will translate into many more dollars and many more family memories down the road.

CHAPTER 12

WHILE WE'RE YOUNG

Everywhere is walking distance if you have the time.

Steven Wright

A few years ago, while standing in the half-price line in Times Square for Broadway theater tickets, I began chatting with the man in front of me. We eventually shared with each other what we did for a living. He was the CEO of a major Canadian company, and we talked a short time about business and finances.

"So what are you doing in this half-price line?" I asked him with a smile, once I felt comfortable that he had a sense of humor. It was clear that he was capable of springing for the full price.

"I was going to ask you the same thing!" he responded. It seems he had surmised that I was capable, too.

Let me offer an educated guess that a contributing factor to his acquisition of wealth came from his thrift. He was not one to overspend, and clearly it was a way of life for him.

It is essential that we pass on to our children, early in life, the lesson that they must live below their means. The best way to teach that to future generations is by modeling that behavior for them. I was modeling this choice by standing in the half-price ticket line.

In that spirit, therefore, I offer this chapter of tidbits of sound advice for younger people. It is good advice at any age, frankly, but if your temples are getting gray and you find yourself wishing your children were reading this book, too, here are some things you might want to share with those you care about.

Preparing Your Children for Success

As I said, I wish I could say it was easy. It wasn't,
but it wasn't hard either. But without a strong
reason or purpose, anything in life is hard.

ROBERT KIVOSAKI

A parent's primary role is to nurture and educate children and prepare them to become independent and successful adults. I think every parent understands and desires this. Not only do you want to launch your children into a fulfilling life, but it is also important to get them off the family payroll.

One of your biggest financial risks is that your children will remain dependent upon you as adults. It is critical that you do all you can to launch them successfully. You need to help fill them with a sense of self-direction and self-worth that leads to them desiring to be financially independent.

Time invested in your children is time well spent. Getting them involved in sports is good, but it is not enough. Listen to them, counsel them, read to them, and give them chores to do around the house. That is how you help them build the skills and relationships that they will need as they face the challenges of adulthood.

Too often the presumption is that once a child has completed high school, it is time for college. But what if your son or daughter does not seem ready for that step? That is the case for many young people. The school counselor may feel that college is the answer, but it really is only you and your child who can make that evaluation.

Statistics show that 59 percent of those who start college will graduate with a bachelor's degree in six years. Some enter college with no plan for the career they might pursue, or their study skills may be seriously deficient. If they are unprepared, they will struggle more than other students, and if they don't get the necessary help, they may eventually drop out with fewer career options.

If you are not sure your child is ready for college or that college is the best choice, there are other options. You may want to consider some alternatives to college or provide them with an opportunity for growth before they take that step. Some young people may be better off working at a full-time job for a while, although ideally it should be one that provides meaningful experiences. It is challenging to find an attractive job with a high school education. Military service certainly can build character, but it requires several years of commitment and, of course, inherent risks. We have seen that many children really just want to work and are not destined for college. For them there are many vocational programs available.

A valuable alternative for some students is a gap year program. These programs provide experiences that help children mature, helping increase the likelihood of collegiate success. Young people may one day look back at this as one of the more fulfilling times of their life. Gap years are relatively common for Europeans. Princeton University even has a "Bridge Year" program that allows a group of incoming freshmen to take a year to work at an international location and gain an international perspective as well as intercultural skills.

Our youngest daughter, Lily, was still seventeen when she graduated from high school. She had the academic skills needed for success in college, but she felt that she wanted to be a year older before she took this next step. She investigated a few gap year programs and chose one called "Where There Be Dragons". The program specialized in skill building through trekking to remote locations and promoting cultural sensitivity by living with families in those areas.

The program got its name from the designation that ancient cartographers often placed on maps at the edge of the known world—"here there be dragons," a region unexperienced and unknown, a place of true adventure. For Lily, that was Bolivia and Peru. In Bolivia, she lived for a month with a family in their modest rural home, trekked in the mountains with the group, and spent time learning about local politics and cultural values. In Peru, she explored more rural areas and visited a village on the Amazon. Lily came home for Christmas and then spent the winter living in Spain with our exchange student, Laura, and her mother, Carmen. She took classes in Spanish and had a wonderful exposure to living in another country and with another family. Living in another city and with another family has its challenges, but Lily gained a great deal from the experience.

As a result, when Lily entered college the next fall she was much more socially mature, and she was conversationally fluent in Spanish. She had also learned about drinking responsibly in a country where it is socially accepted among young people her age. That, too, prepared her to handle the peer pressures of the party atmosphere so prevalent at many American colleges.

I am proud of her, clearly, but I share this to point out the value of such gap year programs. Many children would do well with some extra time to experience life rather than being shuttled straight off to college. There are other good programs that specialize in international education or outdoor skill competency. A web search of "gap year programs" will yield a variety of options. These programs are not inexpensive, but investing in your child's success is of great value. You will find it more expensive if your child tries college for a few years and then drops out. He or she may not be ready for college right away, but it is still essential to be productively engaged in building skills for the future.

Selecting a College

Many parents cherish the dream of their child enrolling at an Ivy League college. Certainly those are amazing schools, and they can be a ticket to great success. The reality is that only a select few will get into those schools. When young people are applying to colleges, their parents should be helping them to discern between price and value. Specifically, they should have real conversations about college costs and what it is all worth.

Our oldest daughter, Natalie, went on college tours and concluded that Kenyon College in Ohio was where she wanted to go. Kenyon said there was no scholarship available for her, and the cost would be $42,000 a year. Natalie was also accepted at Denison University, also in Ohio, and Denison said the cost would be $22,000 a year because the list price was less and Natalie was going to receive a $15,000 scholarship.

We told Natalie that she had a couple of great choices, but we really thought that Kenyon did not offer enough value beyond what Denison did, if any, and that if she really thought that Kenyon was important to her, that she could pay the difference. This was a good lesson. Natalie is responsible, but if you communicate to your children that money is no object, then they will treat it as such. It may take them longer to learn that money needs to be carefully managed. Parents need to talk about these matters openly with their children.

In choosing a private school versus a public school, the information in the marketplace on the matter is generally poor and fails to explain the real issues. When your children graduate from college, the goal is to have them be prepared for a career or at least ready to begin working. In addition to this, we are seeking to have them develop into adults capable of managing their own life and to work well with others. College can be much more than just academics, and as parents we need to look at our children and think about what will assist them in these key development areas. They ultimately must select the college themselves, but your guidance is important.

If your focus begins with cost, private and public schools appear to be vastly different. My first contention is that this is an important factor but should be far from the leading one. Take a close look at what a particular school will do to help your child develop. Is there an opportunity to get to know professors at a more personal level? Do most students live on campus, creating a community for them to participate in? Is this a school where most students come home on weekends? If so, they are much less likely to gain the social experiences that are so beneficial heading into adulthood.

It is also important to separate list price from actual cost. Private schools typically will discount the tuition with significant scholarships for a majority of students that apply. The actual cost for tuition and fees, therefore, typically is between $25,000 and $30,000 for most private, nonprofit universities, with the exception of the costly Ivy League schools and many private colleges on the East Coast. Public in-state universities are typically in the $20,000 to $25,000 range. There's still a gap, but it is not as great as it would appear when you first compare public and private colleges.

What many parents do not recognize when they compare the costs of colleges is that they are not comparing the actual costs for the time it takes to earn a bachelor's degree. Simply put, many public universities have a very poor record of students graduating in four years. At many state schools, six years is more the norm. Only one-third of Michigan schools are graduating enough students in six years to top the national average, which is about 59 percent according to the *Detroit News and the National Center for Education Statistics.*[26] According to a report from Complete College America, at most public universities, only 19 percent of full-time students earn a bachelor's degree in four years.[27] The required courses for a program may not be readily available, and the students struggle to get into the sequential classes that they need to graduate. In other words, often what you are looking at is the difference between your child going to a private college for four years versus going to a public college for five or more years. When that is the case, the price differential narrows.

Overall, you want to consider the relative experience that your child will have in a public college versus a private college. Smaller class sizes and more intensive residential experiences create strong opportunities for growth at private colleges. Many public colleges are seeking to duplicate this type of experience by creating colleges within a college. Each child ultimately typically selects what college is the best fit for them; parents can encourage them to look at all the options before they decide.

---

26 Kim Kozlowski, "College graduation rates lag in Michigan," *Detroit News,* April 26, 2015, http://www.detroitnews.com/story/news/education/2015/04/26/college-graduation-rates-lag-michigan/26429967/.

27 Tamar Lewin, "Most College Students Don't Earn a Degree in 4 Years, Study Finds", *New York Times,* December 1, 2014, http://www.nytimes.com/2014/12/02/education/most-college-students-dont-earn-degree-in-4-years-study-finds.html.

Full disclosure: As I write this book, I am serving as a board member of the Board of Trustees of Alma College, a wonderful liberal arts school in Michigan. I see the success of what the Alma experience creates and so of course have a bias. I realize our public colleges also have great success stories. It is, however, my experience that small colleges have an enviable batting average of creating successful graduates ready to participate fully in careers and life.

Saving for College

I have seen people with modest incomes who have set aside $300 monthly for each of their children from the time they were born. It might seem that amount would never add up, but by the time the child is ready for college, the college account has grown significantly. If they saved $300 a month for eighteen years at a 6 percent rate of return, they would have $125,543. Starting to save at age ten, the same amount saved adds up to just $52,662. Others don't think about the cost until the child is sixteen years old, and you cannot create the money out of thin air. It takes those small deposits growing over time to add up to big money. Projecting a flat return of 6 percent a year is of course not realistic; returns will vary over time based on risks taken and market returns. The cost of college has also gone up significantly over time, so if you saved assuming college costs are static you will find yourself short.

For our youngest daughter, we started out putting $50 a month in a college account. I would agree that's not enough, but we also found a credit card that would pay 2 percent of everything we spent into the college account. I have used the card for business expenses as well, and the result has been a contribution of a few thousand dollars every year into the account. Eighteen years later, with a few additional deposits, the account has grown to $75,000. Saving for college is much more successful if you have time on your side, so start early! [28]

Building a Strong Financial Base

Once they have made it through their college years, many young people today face a mountain of college debt that they will need to incorporate into their planning. Unfortunately, that debt makes it harder for them to set aside money for their future, which they should start doing without delay.

If they have done well in school and are in a field of study that is in demand, they may land a great job and make significant income. It can become easy to adopt a lifestyle in which they spend most of their paycheck. It is important to resist that temptation. This early career period will be one of their greatest opportunities to build liquid assets.

As I look back, it was the money that my wife and I were able to set aside in our twenties that ultimately had much to do with generating a lot of what we have today. You cannot foresee the challenges that you will face in life, and so you need to prepare early.

For example, let's say about twenty years ago I counsel a couple in their twenties that together earned nearly $200,000 a year. I urge them to save, and they attempt to, setting aside a total of approximately $80,000 in investments over a few years.

Fast-forward a decade, and they have four children. They now have purchased a bigger house, and the wife has interrupted her career to be a homemaker. As they adjust to living on a single salary, they have begun to spend their savings. Unfortunately the primary wage earner then loses his job in the downturn of 2008–09. At this point, not much would be left of their financial cushion other than

---

28 This example is for illustrative purposes only. Actual investor results will vary.

a small amount in their Roth IRAs. This couple is now approaching their forties, fraught with anxiety, and wondering how to make ends meet. It did not have to happen that way. If they had saved more when they had higher incomes, they would have been in a much better position to deal with the down cycles of the economy and the inevitable challenges of life.

Their predicament illustrates the importance of building a strong financial base right out of college. You do not need to ramp up your spending. If you think back to your college days, you probably spent $20 a week. Obviously once young people are paying rent and setting up a home, they will be spending more than that, but they should curb extravagant spending.

It is essential that people in their twenties and thirties understand the impact that the decisions they make today will have on their future financial life. Saving for the future needs to be a top priority when you are first independent. It is best to avoid the monthly car payment, full-featured cable bill, most expensive phone plan, expensive vacations, and dining out nightly. If you adopt that lifestyle, before long you will find yourself thirty to forty years old and having squandered years where you really had an opportunity to start building wealth.

I know young people in their twenties who are saving and maximizing their 401(k)s and Roth IRAs. Some have saved $300,000 or $400,000 by the time they reach age thirty. They achieve this by saving the maximum amount of $18,000 in a 401(k) every year and maximizing a Roth contribution of $5,500. Over the next thirty years, that money may increase in value, and this saving will make it far easier for them to withstand the transitions of family and career that virtually everyone faces at some point. They should be financially comfortable. My advice to them would be to make sure that they also contribute to a liquid investment account so that they have cash for that first home and gaps in their career.

Money worries cause people so much stress, but often they have put themselves in that position by their own actions. The recipe for success is rather simple: save more, spend less, and repeat. Eventually you will be worrying less. That is a key message to impart to your children.

So many people spend to the level of what they make, without a thought for the future—and as a result, their future becomes seriously impaired. Again, we don't know what the future holds. If you make the mistake of thinking you will get around to saving someday, you may fall far short when that someday comes, and instead you find yourself laid off from your job and cannot find another that pays nearly as well. You will need money to fill the income gaps in your life.

Here is what can happen if you live paycheck to paycheck, save nothing for retirement, and lack the liquidity to get through tough times. You may have been enjoying a nice lifestyle, but then in your fifties you lose your job. As the months pass you begin to work your way through whatever savings you do have. Perhaps you begin making early withdrawals from your retirement account. Then at age sixty-two, you end up taking your Social Security benefit and subsisting on that and part-time work.

It's hardly anyone's dream retirement, but I have seen it happen to people who were living well in their forties, with good careers and a full household. "Yes, we should start saving soon for retirement," they told themselves. Little did they know how far behind they already were. Life can throw curves. It is essential to prepare early.

Teaching Money Management

Helping young people learn to manage money is an important parental duty. From the time my daughters were age ten or twelve, I had them come into the office with me and help to clean it. I would monitor and supervise their work. I paid them for their work, but I put the money in a Roth retirement account in their names. By the time they graduated from high school, each of them had a solid start on saving in their Roth, and they have continued to invest in it after college. They now have a nice start on retirement.

We also set up Uniform Gift to Minors Act (UGMA) accounts for our children. These accounts can be used to save for college, but when your child turns eighteen or twenty-one, depending on the state, the account is theirs. That means this is not an ideal arrangement if your children become spendthrifts. However, you will be able to quickly see how they handle their money and can begin working to correct any poor habits. As for our children, they knew that the UGMA account was their seed money, and it was there for them when they had to rent their first apartments and faced other expenses. They have not come to us seeking further help.

This book is written with the assumption that you are relatively wealthy and your children will not get need-based aid for college. With that in mind, a UGMA account is not necessarily the right choice if your child will be seeking financial aid for college. The college will expect the young person to use the money in the account for educational purposes. For many people, a 529 plan is a more advantageous college savings account because the money contributed to it grows tax-free, and colleges look at it differently than they look at UGMA accounts that are in the child's name. For wealthy investors, a 529 and its tax-free growth is a real bonus. Additionally, you are demonstrating to your children the benefits of long-term savings.

By whatever means, it is a good idea to put your children in a position so that when they come out of college they do not have to come to you for money. Think of it as a starting point upon which they can build their wealth. If they know they have their seed money and cannot use you as a bank, they will feel more of an incentive to make this work. They will learn to manage money.

Toward that end, I can recommend some good financial management computer programs. One is Mint, an online program particularly useful for young people to monitor their spending over multiple bank accounts and credit cards. As I mentioned earlier, my firm uses a program called eMoney Advisor, which we provide specifically to clients to track their assets, debts, and spending. They can see, in one convenient listing, the comings and goings of their money.

Investing in Marriage

The loss of a spouse can be devastating financially, and often that loss does not involve death—it involves divorce. The risk of a failed marriage is yet another reason to build up resources to get through what is likely to be a turbulent time. Who to marry is one of life's most important decisions. A good choice will lead to a richness of life—emotionally, spiritually, and financially—and, as with anything of great value, it should be nurtured. Invest in your marriage.

Marriage counseling was one of the best investments that Sabrina and I ever made. Anyone who has been married knows that to be wed is not always bliss. I married a wonderful woman, but each of us had issues to address, and we did so when we were in our forties. Counseling helped us move forward with a spirit of empathy.

How sad it is when dreams and plans are tossed away because couples cannot get along. Left unaddressed, misunderstandings can ferment into anger, and once the word "divorce" is spoken, it is hard to take back. The remedy to a misunderstanding, of course, is understanding. You need to understand not only your spouse's heart but your own. Our counselor congratulated us that we had come to her early. She told us that so many couples get to the point where they are no longer talking to each other. It is far better to seek to enrich a marriage rather than wait to see if it can be salvaged.

In general, divorce is often a financial disaster or at least a significant financial setback. Where once there was one home, now there are two, with all the associated maintenance expenses. More expenses mean less savings, and it becomes ever harder to reach retirement goals. In many cases of divorce, each of the former spouses will need to work an additional five to ten years beyond what they had planned.

That is why counseling pays such huge dividends. You are investing in a solid relationship. It makes as much sense financially as it does emotionally and spiritually. I have long recognized the value of being grounded in all three. For years I have spoken monthly with the spiritual advisor Jonathan Ellis, who helps me to think through life's situations. Life can move along quickly at times, and we all need the opportunity to step back and reflect. If you want to reach out to others, you must first be in touch with yourself.

Dealing with Debt

At some time or another, most people decide to make some purchases on credit, whether it is taking out a mortgage for a home or paying with plastic when they go shopping. The question is whether you are buying an appreciating or a depreciating asset. Are you investing in something that will grow in value and make money for you, or are you simply taking on debt for things that eventually will be worth little or nothing?

There is no good credit card debt. If you use a card, you should pay it off every month. Otherwise, you are likely to see the balance growing and feel caught in a high-interest trap. And since nothing that you are purchasing has the potential to gain in value, this is not the kind of debt that you can leverage to your advantage.

When purchasing cars, we simply look at the rates the auto companies offer versus what we can make on our investments. Generally, auto loans are available at very low rates. If the rate is low, I have taken a loan when purchasing vehicles. If the rates go higher in the future, I will purchase cars with cash. For younger people, that may not be an option. I would encourage them to agree to a loan that is for a shorter period than the total length of time they expect to own the car. For example, a four-year loan agreement makes sense if you plan to own the car for eight years.

Traditionally, a house has been a purchase that will gain in value, and therefore a house has long been considered a reliable investment. It certainly has worked out well for many people over the years as a way to build wealth. Sabrina and I learned much about budgeting when we bought our first house. We learned the discipline of setting money aside to take care of household expenses, and as we made our payments, we built equity that served us well.

Our first house, in Ann Arbor, was relatively modest and cost $85,000. We had looked at more expensive houses but decided to keep the payments lower. When I began my career as a financial advisor, my income, too, was modest, so those lower payments made it easier to get through the next few years. Nor did we have car payments. Sabrina returned to work part-time, and because our expenses were low, we had enough to get by while I built my business. I don't know that it would have been possible if we had been living in a $400,000 house and were burdened with loans. By living modestly, we gained flexibility. When younger people get committed to high fixed investments, they lose much of that flexibility.

Many Americans are over-housed, reaching beyond their means to buy the most expensive accommodations that they are able to qualify for. I recognize that housing costs are a challenge on both of the American coasts and in many cities. The house becomes a drag on resources that prevents people from saving what they need to. If you were to meet many of my clients, you would notice that their houses are far less expensive than they have been told they can afford. They are nice but not overly elaborate. These are wealthy people, and I am sure that living within their means contributed to their success.

That is not the message you are likely to hear from a real estate agent who makes a larger commission by selling more expensive homes. After years of rapidly increasing housing prices, many people concluded that the more they spent for a house, the more they would benefit from the rising prices. It didn't seem to be all that much of a risk, but that risk became clear as we saw the plunge in home prices in 2008–09 and the wave of mortgage defaults. But it is not this risk of declining home prices that is your greatest risk when purchasing an expensive home. It is the ongoing costs that prevent you from being able to save. Mortgage payments, heating and cooling, repairs, furniture, taxes, and so on—all these costs accumulate and over decades can significantly impede your ability to save and live within your means.

To illustrate this, let's imagine a client with a million-dollar primary home and a million-dollar lakefront second home in the early 2000s. He is earning over $500,000 annually, before stock options, so he and his wife believe that they can afford the expense. However, they are spending the majority of their income to pay the mortgage, taxes, and maintenance on two fine homes. They are simply not saving. Unfortunately, in the 2008 downturn, he loses his job. Meanwhile, the market crisis meant that his stock options had no value, and the two houses declined in value and debt on them actually exceeded their value. To sell them would have been difficult, as well as unwise.

In this example, the client is able to arrange some consulting work and has the benefit of a large pension, so this couple does not go bankrupt. But the situation certainly would be very uncomfortable, and their inability to afford these homes would bring them years of stress. Their predicament illustrates the need to avoid overspending. If instead they had owned a $400,000 home and $300,000 cottage, they could have easily made the payments while also saving money. The downturn would not have hurt so much. Even wealthy people should consider whether they are saving money every year or are drawing on their savings. If the answer is *drawing on savings,* they need to make adjustments, or that wealth will dissipate much faster than people think.

Winning the Race

In 1977, the year I graduated from college, I bought a sixteen-foot Hobie Cat catamaran. I had sailed for many years but never in a boat with the power and speed of the Hobie, a thoroughbred of small boat racing. I began racing it regularly on Sand Lake, where my parents had a cottage, competing with a small group of avid Hobie owners. We had races on the Fourth of July and Labor Day.

I competed for years—decades, actually—but I rarely won. The trophy moved from cottage to cottage but seldom to ours. But I continued to sail, sometimes pulling my daughters and her friends behind the boat on a line—they called it "dragging." Over time, my skills improved to the point that today, the trophy usually resides in our cottage.

That success, as with so much else in life, came from a desire to get into the race and persistently pursue the goal over time. That boat cost me $1,500—it wasn't a new one, which would have cost several times more—and I got a four-installment loan from a bank to pay it off quickly. Though I agree that young people should spend cautiously, I must say that was the best money I ever spent. I was buying more than the boat. I was buying memories. I was buying joyous hours with friends out on the water.

And that is the balance we all need in life. As parents impart the details of good financial management to young people, it is important to keep a perspective on the value not only of dollars but also of dreams. We win the race when we lead a fulfilling life.

CONCLUSION

PURSUIT OF HAPPINESS

Don't confuse motion and progress. A rocking horse
keeps moving but doesn't make any progress.

ALFRED A. MONTAPERT

If it feels like you're on a rocking horse, going nowhere, you
need to redefine what being productive means to you. Even the
smartest people make the mistake of assuming that motion is
equal to action. Instead of doing more things to achieve your goals,
do things that have more of an impact on making progress.

PATRICK ALLAN

"Dad, I'm going on a three-day fast—would you like to join me?" my daughter Natalie asked me one day. She had been doing some reading on the health benefits. I had rarely missed a meal in years, but I agreed to give it a try.

On the first day I felt pretty good—a little weak later in the day but not exceptionally hungry. On the second day, I was less active but felt all right. I just drank water and had a little tea. On the third day, I had a lot of energy and did a lot of work around our lake cottage. I didn't feel hungry at all.

The experience was eye-opening for me. I gained a new appreciation for the fact that you really don't have to eat all the time—that just drinking water is adequate in the short run. We often eat by reflex, thinking we need a meal every day at specified intervals, even when in truth we could do without. I have recognized that the impulse is mostly just a matter of desire and can be ignored.

We need to keep our minds open to possibilities. This is not to say that I am advocating a starvation diet if things get tough. But I am saying that things are not always as they seem. If you have millions, you might think people who live paycheck to paycheck must be unhappy, but that's not necessarily the case. They are probably no less happy than you. So much depends upon attitude, perspective, and a supportive safety net.

As my financial practice grew, I was able to move my family to a bigger house, the one on the pond where we skate. Our previous house in Ann Arbor was more modest, but our children didn't see it that way. It was their time with other children in the neighborhood that made their life rich, and that joy didn't arise from a bigger house with more belongings. It came from the relationships they nurtured, whether in town or out on the lake.

People often imagine some magical and wonderful thing will happen when they achieve a certain level of wealth. What they need to realize is the importance of enjoying life daily. Otherwise they risk missing so much along the way. Those who live within their means, even when their means are modest, can have a great life, free of stress. People who stretch their budget to pursue life's luxuries, spending everything they make without saving, inevitably will feel the strain. They're always pushing for more stuff without finding meaning in it.

It's a distortion of the American dream to pursue money without purpose. It's time to step back. Do you truly need all the things you strive to acquire? Those material possessions are the emblems of getting ahead, but in and of themselves they do not mean that you truly have gotten ahead. The only way to do that is to live within your means, and in time your wealth will grow, as will your sense of security.

Challenges will surely come your way. When you have been building your wealth, you will be in a much better position to handle the challenges. You will be able to handle the rough patches or lend a hand to loved ones when they face difficulties. We are here to help one another. We need to extend a spirit of generosity to others, and we need to reach out to others when we ourselves need help.

Once, when Audrey was about eight, we were on a Florida beach vacation and I took a phone call from a client. The call was not all that critical, but it lasted an hour. "Dad!" she protested when I hung up. "This is vacation. You're supposed to be spending time with us!" Years later, I still think about that. We should listen to the wisdom of children. We owe them our time. The workaday world with its ringing phones and rivers of e-mails can wait.

Wealth can be defined in many ways, but it comes down to living well. We need to find the right balance between work and life. No matter how much longer people live these days, life is still short. We must not squander the hours we have been given. In the end, that's why we work hard, invest wisely, and save for the future. We are in pursuit of happiness.

A S   I   S E E   I T

SOME THOUGHTS FROM

THE AUTHOR

Every author, upon completing a book, invariably ends up with a file of notes and passages that didn't seem to fit within the flow of the chapters. In my case, I found that these "leftovers" amounted to a compendium of my opinions on various matters. Rather than discard them, I have decided to offer some of them to you here in an appendix. And so, for what it's worth, here's how I see it...

The reason I am writing this chapter is a reflection of my concerns about the future of America. These comments are not about social issues but financial ones. As a country we face the same issues individuals do. We can't overspend, we need to save for a rainy day, and we need to manage our resources responsibly. Governments are in many cases able to put off the day of reckoning much longer than individuals can. They can borrow money when they should not be able to simply because bond holders see them as having taxing authority to get them through difficult times. As a result, governments rarely fail, but when they do, it typically devastates the finances of all the citizens. One only needs to look at places like Venezuela, Argentina, and Russia. In each case, extreme inflation is a common result of excessive government spending, and this inflation is awful for citizens and their financial futures.

How we treat those less fortunate than us is a real measure of who we are. We need to seek to make a difference in our world, and fixing government polices has the potential to improve the lives of all.

On Government Services and Regulation

Working in financial services for over twenty years, I have seen the spectrum of how wealth can be accumulated as well as dissipated. In the small Michigan town where I grew up in the 1960s, our neighborhood contained families from all walks of life, and the standard of living for all was relatively similar. Today, life in America is far different. The upper class generally lives in affluent neighborhoods, while those with fewer resources live in the country, apartments, or trailers. The less educated do not get the job opportunities to provide the standard of living that they once could have. The best jobs are hard to come by. For our society to continue to thrive overall, we need participation by all. Those in the lower income ranges need protections in place so that they can have quality lives with less income.

Here I will share some of my thoughts on three reforms I see as key to the success of the lower middle class and society at large. A key role of government is to have a safety net for the lower middle class and poor. The wealthy have the resources to overcome burdensome government regulations or expensive health care, but the less fortunate do not. Here are my thoughts on what we need to fix, based on what I have seen in my years of looking at people's finances.

Reforming the Income Tax Code

A primary duty of government is to allow honest people to predict the result of their own conduct. Today, before you complete your tax return, even a CPA will have difficulty estimating your tax liability.

This is far from allowing honest people to predict the result of their own conduct. Preparing a tax return is a real burden for poor people and a convoluted exercise for the wealthy. The complexity of the tax code also makes all kinds of decisions much more complex than if an individual's income were simply taxed with no deductions. Should you buy or rent a home? Without tax deductions, it is simple: What is the monthly cost? Currently you need to figure in your deductions for interest and property taxes and whatever other breaks you might get as a homeowner.

Citizens should know that the money in their pocket from their paycheck is theirs, and once it is paid to them, they no longer owe taxes on it. For most people, they should never have to file a tax return unless they work for themselves and need to calculate their income. Filing a tax return should be an opportunity to get money back because you have had some exceptional circumstance of costs or have given a truly extraordinary amount to charity.

We need to reform our tax system along the lines of what New Zealand and a number of other countries have done:

- Taxes are withheld from pay on a progressive basis; the more you earn, the more that is withheld.
- Taxes on dividends and interest are withheld at the source by banks and corporations.
- There are almost no deductions and 90 percent of the people never file a tax return. Politicians no longer spend time arguing for special benefits for homeowners, people in high-tax states, sales tax, etc. Without deductions, there are no benefits to argue about and the ability of our legislators to squander our resources with special deals becomes more limited. The government would have to phase out current deductions over time since people have, for example,

purchased homes counting on a mortgage deduction. But the only way to reform is to make the changes and phase them in so that eventually we are on a more logical system. Although we clearly spend a lot of time working on helping clients with tax strategies, a much simpler tax code will not eliminate opportunities to invest in a tax-efficient manner or to better strategize about building and preserving wealth.

Reform of Delivery of Health Care

The runaway cost of health care and lack of an affordable health-care safety net for the poor is one of the most significant risks to our society today. In most Western nations, health care is provided as a basic service to all. The cost of health care in those societies runs typically from 7 to 12 percent of gross domestic product (GDP). Many will argue that people have to wait for service or there are other issues, but generally people in those countries find the service acceptable.

In the United States, health care costs us close to 20 percent of GDP, and people at the margins are poorly served, struggling to navigate the system and always at risk of bankruptcy as they face those runaway costs. The Affordable Care Act of 2010 was an effort to change this but really was just a patch on the current system. Ultimately it has not contained costs and is proving to be unaffordable. Today, the cost of health care for a family of four in America is $24,671.[29] When health care costs $24,000 a year, it is not devastating financially if you are making $200,000 a year. If you are making $50,000 a year, it is. What is the solution?

---

29 Dan Munro, "Annual Healthcare Costs For Family Of Four Now At $24,671," *Forbes*, May 19, 2015, http://www.forbes.com/sites/danmunro/2015/05/19/annual-healthcare-cost-for-family-of-four-now-at-24671/#6769c0f64dfb.

- Build a system that mimics what has been done successfully in other countries. Governments providing medical services in other countries are doing this at a dramatically lower cost to GDP.

- Implement national health care, with employees working for the government delivering the services.

Many will argue that the government is never the most efficient provider of services, and I would not dispute this. But we have to recognize that our current approach is not working and try some other radical solution. I am reminded of the one definition of insanity: Doing the same thing over and over again and expecting a different result.

- Wealthy individuals (such as my clients) might think, *I don't want to be subject to government health care and someone denying me treatment.* My argument is simply that this will not be your only option. You will have private insurance as a supplement, and if you need service and cannot wait, you will get it through your private insurance.

- The current crisis in the cost of health care has really worsened as a result of insurance. Because of insurance, people do not shop for best price. If you ask medical providers what a procedure costs, they can almost never tell you. They simply do not know. As a result the normal process of people pricing services that constrains pricing in most industries does not exist. The cost of a similar medical procedure will vary widely across the country and even within neighboring counties. What is the rationale for this?

- The cost of drugs is also an important factor. Although a relatively small part of the overall cost, it is rising quickly as the pharmaceutical industry has seen very little real pushback to rapid increases in drug prices. We have dramatically higher drug costs than Canada and most other first-world countries. In the long run, our citizens cannot afford this.

U.S. Spending on Healthcare

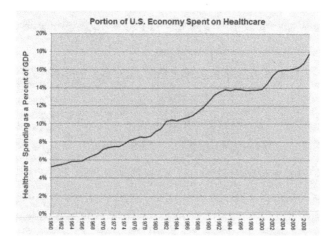

Portion of U.S. Economy Spent on Healthcare

irce: U.S. Department of Health & Human Services, Centers for Medicare and Medicaid Services
P = Gross Domestic Product which measures the amounts of goods and services produced within a given country

38

Reforming Public Employee Benefits

I live in Ann Arbor, a prosperous city in Michigan and home to the University of Michigan. At one time the city was an affordable place for those of modest means to live. Today that is no longer the case. High property taxes, used primarily to pay the cost of running the city, are driving up the cost of living. What are the biggest costs of running the city? Payroll and retirement benefits are the vast majority of the annual budget. My window into this is serving public employees and seeing their benefits as part of my retirement planning for them.

There is no question in my mind that these individuals worked hard and were good public servants. My question is simply whether the benefits we are offering to them are comparable to what individuals in the private sector earn and whether they are affordable to the public. Unfortunately, the answer is *no*. The benefits were ratcheted up to compete with auto industry employees, who at one time had amazing benefits. Those employees no longer have these benefits, but public employees still do. The benefits bankrupted the auto companies (GM and Chrysler went bankrupt in 2008), and they were a key factor in bankrupting the city of Detroit. In time, they may bankrupt many other cities and states in America. Chicago and Illinois are in real trouble as I write this.

In theory, pension benefits are funded during a person's working career, so the taxpayer who is benefiting from the employee's work is paying the cost. What has actually happened in the recent past is that the funding has not kept up with the costs, and in many cases the result is that benefits are being funded by new taxpayers who may never have been served by these workers. Health care is a second retirement benefit that was once a modest part of the cost to a municipality. When people retire in their early fifties and live into their eighties or older, health care is no longer a modest retirement cost. Health care now becomes a burden on current taxpayers to pay the health-care cost of retirees who similarly never served them.

A Michigan study on unfunded health-care costs released in 2013 gave some sense of the worsening crisis. It seems Detroit was not alone: More than three hundred other communities representing two-thirds of the state's residents were facing unfunded health-care liabilities of $12.7 billion in the next three decades. Ultimately these costs that are passed on to taxpayers make it simply unaffordable for the poor and lower middle class to live in our cities in anything other than subsidized housing. The high costs of public employee's retirement benefits also reduce the number of public jobs, with cities continually cutting back staffing and city services suffering. A decade ago, Ann Arbor had over 1,100 employees—today there are closer to seven hundred, and the costs of employees are higher than they were a decade ago.

One only needs to look at the state of roads and infrastructure in the country to understand that if payroll and benefit costs are out of control, then the money is coming from somewhere. One place the money is coming out of is infrastructure spending, which is actually critical to the poor. Underfunded public services have a major impact on the poor. They are dependent on public buses and subways to get to work. When cities do not have the money, these services suffer. The wealthy drive their cars and put up with the traffic. Ultimately all of us suffer when money is not spent on infrastructure. Fewer public employees and reduced public services—these are the results of excessive benefits.

Solutions to the Public Employee Benefit Crisis

Plan administrators tell the public that investment returns will help resolve the pension crisis. Unfortunately, we are actually entering a period with significantly lower expected investment returns than in the past. Many pension benefits were beefed up after the decades of the eighties and nineties when stocks and bonds were returning 10 percent to 15 percent a year. Most plans today assume returns in the 7 percent range, but with bond yields in the 2 percent to 3 percent range, 7 percent is hard to achieve. Pensions are an important benefit, and in my ideal world they would be a benefit of every job. That's the case, to some extent, in that Social Security is really a type of pension scheme. In order to make public pensions economically viable, provide jobs for the future, and ensure that taxpayer money is being spent wisely, four main issues need to be addressed.

1. The pension formula

Problem: The formula in itself is not bad (you earn a 1 percent benefit of wages for example for each year you work), but in many plans it is so costly that it forces sacrifices for new employees and potential hires. For example, California police earn a 3 percent benefit and after thirty years would get a lifetime pension of 90 percent of wages. Municipalities cannot afford to have employees start working at twenty-two, retire at fifty-two, and get paid 90 percent of wages until they die!

Solution: This problem could be solved by either lowering accrual rates, capping pensions at a certain percent, or some combination of the two. Our typical client retiree lives on 60 to 70 percent of their per retirement wages. A pension capped at 30 percent, along with Social Security providing 20 to 25 percent of annual income, would put public employees in a far better position than most Americans and would require them to save enough themselves to provide them an additional 20 percent of their income.

2. Pension spiking

Problem: The practice of including overtime, unused sick leave, and longevity pay—among other things—

when calculating final average salary has cost governments thousands of dollars per retiree each year. For example, the California retiree is earning $80,000 a year, but the pension is based on average wages in the last three years. So the worker might generate a lot of overtime and other wages to plump up the average wage figure. In Ann Arbor the routine is to promote many employees to top positions in their last years, spiking their benefits. Some say a fireman in Ann Arbor almost always retires as a chief, if not as a lieutenant. Their wages are much higher in the last few years, and so benefits are much higher.

Solution: Adopting a five- to ten-year formula and only counting base salary when calculating final average compensation.

3. Health benefits

Problem: Many public employees receive extremely generous health-care benefits while employed and throughout retirement, resulting in costs that rival those of the pensions themselves.

Solution: Health-care benefits for public employees need to be brought more in line with those in the private sector in order for it to be affordable for the state and local governments. For most Americans, Medicare is our retirement health-care system, so why is it not for public employees? A national health-care program would also have the potential to dramatically reduce these costs.

4. Retirement ages

Problem: Early retirement means public employees are working for fewer years than in the past but are drawing a pension longer than ever.

Solution: A retiree's benefits should be brought in line with their contributions. Raising the retirement age and limiting early retirement options will help accomplish this. Social Security reduces retiree benefits if you retire early. Very few public pension plans treat employees similarly.

Conclusion: Ultimately our society needs to decide what reasonable and affordable retirement benefits are for public servants. They have logically negotiated to get the best benefits possible. We now need to step back and ask ourselves if the benefits as they are structured today are competitive with the private sector and affordable for our society. I clearly don't think that's the case.

We have an obligation to pay the benefits employees have earned to date. However, we must have the ability to modify those benefits not yet earned. The private sector has recognized that pension benefits may be unaffordable and modified them for both current and new employees. The public sector must do the same.

Lower-middle-class Americans face a future where they may never retire or will eventually stop working and live on just Social Security. Many in middle-class America need to extend their working careers from sixty-five to seventy, hoping to achieve even a modest retirement. At the same time, public servants are retiring in their early to midfifties with lifetime pensions and comprehensive health care that make them among the wealthiest of retirees, while public services and infrastructure suffer from a lack of funds. Is it equitable that nongovernment workers need to work longer so that government workers can retire earlier?

Clearly these three issues—taxation, public health care, and public employee benefits—will not solve all of America's problems. They are, however, important issues that, if left unaddressed, will continue to hamper our ability as a society to prosper and compete on the world stage. Our country has been blessed with wonderful resources, most of all an educated and hardworking populace. Over time we will be challenged unless we resolve these issues.

The information contained in this book does not purport to be a complete description of the securities, markets, or developments referred to in this material. The information has been obtained from sources considered to be reliable, but we do not guarantee that the foregoing material is accurate or complete. Any information is not a complete summary or statement of all available data necessary for making an investment decision and does not constitute a recommendation. Any opinions of the chapter authors are those of the chapter author and not necessarily those of RJFS or Raymond James. Expressions of opinion are as of the initial book publishing date and are subject to change without notice.

Raymond James Financial Services, Inc. is not responsible for the consequences of any particular transaction or investment decision based on the content of this book. All financial, retirement, and estate planning should be individualized, as each person's situation is unique.

This information is not intended as a solicitation or an offer to buy or sell any security referred to herein. Keep in mind that there is no assurance that our recommendations or strategies will ultimately be successful or profitable or protect against a loss. There may also be the potential for missed growth opportunities that may occur after the sale of an investment.

Recommendations, specific investments or strategies discussed may not be suitable for all investors. Past performance may not be indicative of future results. You should discuss any tax or legal matters with the appropriate professional.